Typography: Formation+TransFormation

What can be said at all can be said clearly; and whereof one cannot speak thereof one must be silent.

Ludwig Wittgenstein (1889–1951)

Willi Kunz

Typography: Formation + TransFormation

Niggli

Printed in Switzerland
ISBN 3-7212-0495-6

Published by
Verlag Niggli AG
Steinackerstrasse 8
8583 Sulgen
Switzerland

English edition
available from

Willi Kunz Books
PO Box 282
Planetarium Station
New York, NY 10024-0282
212 799 4300
212 877 7024 fax
wkany@aol.com

I would like to thank Shannon Ford for meticulous editing and valuable suggestions in clarifying the text, and the publisher, Verlag Niggli AG, for their commitment to produce again a high-quality book.

Many thanks also go to the readers of my book, *Typography: Macro- and Microaesthetics* first published in 1998. With editions in German and Chinese the volume has found its way into many typography classes. It is most gratifying to know that the text will guide a new generation of typographic designers in continuing the modern project.

For a broader understanding of the typographic principles expounded in my work, I encourage readers to consult my previously published book, *Typography: Macro- and Microaesthetics* which includes the following topics:

Part one discusses the typographic elements; the microaesthetic qualities of letters, numbers, and punctuation marks, lines, and geometric elements and their diverse applications.

Part two analyzes the design aspects of space, structure, sequence, contrast, form and counterform, and illustrates their function with examples from teaching and praxis.

Part three demonstrates how typographic elements contribute to design on the microaesthetic level.

Part four, based on a series of architectural posters, analyzes the interrelationship between purpose, macrostructure, and microaesthetics.

Introduction

On my way to work I pass the Natural History Museum, an imposing neoclassical building. Above the entrance, chiseled in stone in monumental capital letters, appear the words Truth, Knowledge, and Vision – three powerful concepts that provoke contemplation.

Who chose these words? Why did they choose these particular words? Are these words still relevant today? Which of the three words is the most important? Why are they arranged in this particular sequence? How many letters are in each word? What is the ratio between the numbers of letters in each word? What is the total number of letters? How many rectilinear, triangular, and curvilinear letters are in each word? What is the typeface? How tall are the letters? How does the chisel technique contribute to the letter's appearance? How would the words appear in upper and lower case?

These kinds of questions are at the core of a typographic designer's work. They show how a seemingly simple message can be deconstructed to reveal the numerous decisions that together affect the meaning and emotional tone of the communication.

Typography is the major component of visual communication, from books to posters, signs, packaging, magazines, newspapers, and electronic media. A huge amount of information, such as forms, lists, and schedules, is entirely typographically based. We are inundated with typography. Some of it is effective, but much is confusing, amounting to a mere nuisance that is instantly discarded. Because typographic design is ubiquitous, it seems a simple task. Anyone who communicates makes typography.

The basic elements that a typographic designer works with are letters, numbers, and punctuation marks. The twenty-six letters have been part of our memory since early childhood. By themselves, however, letters lack meaning and are incapable of transmitting information. Combined into a word, a series of letters can be very powerful, more precise than a picture. A physical condition like thirst, for instance, is better conveyed with a word than through an image.

Although letters, numbers, and punctuation marks are the basic material a designer works with, typography depends on additional elements, such as space, color, and typefaces to convey meaning. These elements communicate on two interrelated levels: the macroaesthetic and the microaesthetic. The macroaesthetic level includes the primary visual components that are recognized first: the size and proportion of the space; form, composition, and the color of key elements; the structure as a whole; and the contrast between the primary components and the space around them.

The microaesthetic level encompasses the form, size, weight, and relationship of secondary elements: typeface characteristics; letterforms and counter forms; and the spacing between letters, words, lines, and other graphic elements.

The function of typography is to communicate a message's intellectual meaning as well as its emotional tone. Both aspects are necessary for the message to be effective. Letters and punctuation, word sequences, and spatial relationships all perform a utilitarian function in conveying the "facts" of the message. The nuances of a message, where the designer expands its intellectual content and introduces the desired emotional tone, comes primarily from the skilled and sensitive use of these elements. Without utility, the message is useless because it cannot be comprehended. Without emotional tone, the message is ineffective because it does not engage the reader.

Typographic information occupies two-dimensional space. The third dimension is time, the time necessary for the reader to comprehend the information. The more complex the composition, the more time and effort required for comprehension. Every person has a different tolerance for the length of a text. The reader loses interest and tires quickly when the text is too long and monotonous, exceeding his capacity to concentrate and focus. Conveying information in the shortest amount of time and in a visually enticing way is an important goal.

The designer to some extent controls the reader's time. Through the skilful use of typographic materials and space the designer reduces the reader's resistance to text. Intervals between the typographic elements contribute significantly to the visual qualities of design and influence the time required for reading. Ideally, the intervals derive from the structure of the text and are not imposed by the designer.

Typography is many things, to many people. Typographic design is a field that divides into small interest groups including traditionalists, revivalists, rationalists, constructivists, de-constructivists, modernists, post-modernists, and techno freaks, among others. Each group pursues typographic design in a different way. The result is an enormously diverse, constantly changing typographic landscape.

Regardless of what style is pursued, an important criterion in evaluating a design is clarity. Good typography is clear typography. The designer's intent must be immediately clear and the design must speak with an unmistakable, clear voice that penetrates today's clamorous visual environment.

Clear typography is frugal and restrained; it is produced with an economic use of materials and resources. Too many variations and indiscriminate use of typefaces, sizes, weights, alignments, space and color lead to unfocused, confusing results. Compared to the work produced today with unlimited resources and unprecedented technical finesse, the printed artifacts from the 1920s and 1930s – when materials were scarce – appear powerful and convincing. The simple means available then forced the designer to use his imagination and come up with new visual ideas.

High standards derive from a selective process that eliminates the superfluous and ordinary, leaving the essential and extraordinary. By working with voluntary limitations on the visual material we use to express an idea we can concentrate on developing our own unique variations on a typographic theme.

The typographic designer works primarily with existing elements. He rarely creates the typographic material he uses, which works against his disposition. Most designers are driven by creative ambitions. Creativity alone, however, is not sufficient to succeed.

Typographic design is practiced in a fast paced environment, under conditions that distract from the careful study of information and thoughtful development of ideas. To function effectively, the designer needs sound knowledge of communication theory, a good grasp of design principles, an understanding of the intended audience, and a clear focus on the goals of the communications. The more complete our knowledge, and the more fluent we are in the principles of typography, the more we can accomplish in a limited amount of time. The ultimate condition for good typography, however, is a good text.

Typographic design is a visual activity. As such, visual fluency in the components of written language – letters, words, sentences, spelling, grammar, and syntax structure – is required. After we master the components, we are able to create different solutions to a wide range of typographic problems.

However, to succeed, a design must also have a strong intellectual component. Aesthetic qualities are not enough to sustain the reader's interest. The critical reader is looking for an intellectual connection between the content of a message and how it is expressed. The challenge for the designer is to develop an appropriate intellectual component – a theory – as a base for the aesthetics. Theory is often dismissed as too intellectual, too far removed from practice. However, there is no difference between theory and practice. Every design has a theoretical base; in the end, the theory behind it may be obscured but traces of it always remain.

Typographic design involves making decisions. We carefully evaluate different options before deciding which of the possible designs communicates best. It requires organized thinking and an intellectual grasp of the facts pertaining to the design problem. If a problem can be precisely defined, it can be correctly solved. Reducing the available options to a manageable number requires making choices.

In typography the choices we make have a strong impact on design. A particular format, typeface, type size, interline space, composition, color, type of paper, etc. contribute to the quality and expression of a design.

Having too many choices can be overwhelming. Today, the abundance of choices is most obvious in the ever-expanding variety of typefaces. Many designers believe that by choosing a particular typeface the work will significantly change. Variety in typography, however, is not so much determined by the chosen typeface as by the arrangement of text within the chosen format.

Making the right choice requires extensive study, experience and practice. In good typographic design every decision or choice we make is consistent with the design objectives set out at the beginning. If the choices are logical and consistent with the objectives, the final design is cohesive and effective.

Making choices is difficult because good ideas and directions must sometimes be eliminated to arrive at a final solution. Making choices is the moment of truth. In evaluating our work, we have to be honest about its qualities. Does it measure up to the highest standards? Is it the best result we can achieve? The final choice inevitably leaves us ambivalent because it is almost impossible to determine whether the chosen design is the best.

Inherent in typographic design are many uncertainties. At the start there is uncertainty about the elements to choose: format, typeface, type size, color, etc., and the formal aspects of structure, sequence, contrast, proportion, rhythm, composition, form and counter form. Then there is uncertainty about the time invested, about the result of our efforts, and about the client's reaction. To master these uncertainties the designer needs an open, divergent mind-set.

Our intellectual and visual capacities must be honed every day by observing our surroundings, by being interested in related disciplines such as architecture, painting, and film, by challenging the status quo, and by asking critical questions like: how can we reduce waste and visual clutter, improve efficiency, create a better world?

Finding a typographic solution in many instances is not a matter of ideas but of intensive work and commitment. We do extensive research and collect relevant material and facts pertaining to the problem. In the collected material we hope to find the seed to an appropriate conceptual idea.

The old adage "practice creates the master" still has resonance. Personal experimentation and learning from mistakes is much more valuable than looking at design annuals and magazines. Artist's biographies and autobiographies, which reveal the connection between someone's life and work, are a great inspiration.

Without a solid foundation the most creative idea will not be realized successfully. However, even creativity combined with theoretical and technical knowledge is not quite enough. The designer must be driven by an urge to be a pioneer. To find new territory and to develop genuine new ideas we must know the past but concentrate on the future.

In creating any kind of visual communication, typographic material is inexhaustible when used with imagination and skill. After years of practice, I am still fascinated and challenged by the endless variety of visual expressions that can be created with the limited set of typographic elements.

By absorbing the technical facts and learning a few standard tricks, the inexperienced designer can achieve decent results in a relatively short period of time. The results, however, lack depth, and the designer is lost when confronted with a new problem.

A designer should be able to function in any situation; he must be an excellent generalist. He must acquire a core knowledge from which he can branch off in any direction he chooses.

He must be able to develop an appropriate solution from the given economic, social and technical conditions and not impose a formula that has no relation to the problem. Typography has certain principles but no formulas that can be universally applied.

The typographic designer relies on divergent thinking as opposed to the routine thinking practiced daily by the average person. Routine thinking proceeds along a known path with a clear destination. The goal is to attain a predictable result with minimal effort in the shortest amount of time. Divergent thinking is needed to deal with the economic, social and technical demands that are difficult to define in advance and often change during the course of design.

Today, computer technology is ubiquitous; it controls our lives. Electronic equipment has replaced the traditional tools of expression: pencil, crayon, pen, and brush. The tactile qualities of materials such as tracing- and colored paper, boards, and overlay film that often were a source of inspiration are no longer deemed an essential component in developing a design. I first became aware of these changes several years ago, when the art supply store closed my account because I did not purchase enough materials to reach the quarterly minimum charge.

Technological changes and competition have eliminated many graphic professions. The typesetter, letterpress printer, silk screener, sign painter, and repro photographer are a few of the early casualties of the new electronic technologies. These changes will continue at an accelerating pace and will drastically transform typographic communication. Information is increasingly produced by technically trained people without formal education in typographic design. In an age where speed of production is the overriding criteria the typographic designer is constantly losing ground to the technical experts.

Bombarded with propaganda, it is easy to assume that a computer equipped with the right software is all that is needed to succeed. The typographic designer must resist thinking that with a computer, he can create solutions without much personal effort or engagement. The more sophisticated and powerful the electronic tools, the more carefully we must think about the impact they have on the way we design, and the more diligent we must be not to let the tools overrule human creativity, truth, knowledge, and vision.

Survey of typographic variations. The choices we make determine the visual quality of typography, including legibility and readability.

Background	Letter	Word	Line	Paragraph	Column
Shape	**Case**	**Letterspace**	**Word space**	**Alignment**	**Number**
vertical	upper	track 0	uniform	flush left, ragged right	single
horizontal	lower	track +	varied	flush right, ragged left	multiple
square		track –		justified	
triangular	**Face**		**Length**	centered	**Width**
circular	sans serif	**Kerning**	narrow	free form	uniform
rhombic	serif	uniform	medium		varied
hybrid	script	adjusted	wide	**Interline space**	
	decorative			solid	**Placement**
Color		**Baseline**	**Direction**	moderate	centered
white	**Slant**	uniform	horizontal	open	asymmetric
grey	roman	shifted	vertical		
black	italic		slanted	**First line**	**Interline space**
chromatic				flush	uniform
	Weight			indented	varied
Surface	light			extended	
smooth	regular				**Length**
textured	medium				justified
folded	bold				ragged
	Width				
	regular				
	condensed				
	expanded				
	Size				
	text, 6–12 point				
	display, 14–60 point				

1

Formation of information

Typographic design begins with a set of information and a concept. The designer, facing a blank sheet of paper or a computer screen, is anxious about the first step to take in developing a design.

The elements of typography are an obvious starting point, but often do not get the attention they deserve. On a certain level, letterforms are too familiar to provoke deep contemplation.

A thorough understanding of how letters, words, lines, paragraphs and columns are formed, what makes them unique as design elements, and how they express character and emotion are the most essential tools in the designer's repertoire.

The designer with only a cursory understanding of the elements of typography lacks a base; he misses the opportunity to use them as a springboard to design solutions.

The basic components of letterforms are horizontal, vertical, slanted, and curvilinear strokes.

Combined, strokes imply elementary letterforms.

Creating letterforms

Each of the 26 upper and lower case letters has a distinct structure, which determines the letter's meaning. If the structure deviates significantly from its common form, the letter no longer communicates. It loses its function.

Each letter's structure consists of a certain number of strokes. There are four types of strokes: vertical, horizontal, slanted, and curvilinear. Each stroke has a specific optical quality. The vertical stroke appears unstable, as if suspended in space. The horizontal stroke is stable, integrating into the flow of reading. The slanted stroke is ambivalent; it stands in strong contrast to the predominantly horizontal and vertical composition of typography. The curvilinear stroke is expansive; its expression ranges from a short curve to a slow, long arch. A curve with a consistent radius is circular; with a changing radius, elliptical.

When strokes combine, their optical quality coalesces into a new form. A vertical and a horizontal stroke joined at 90 degrees imply a T or an L; combining a vertical and a slanted stroke suggests an N; a vertical and a curvilinear stroke form a D.

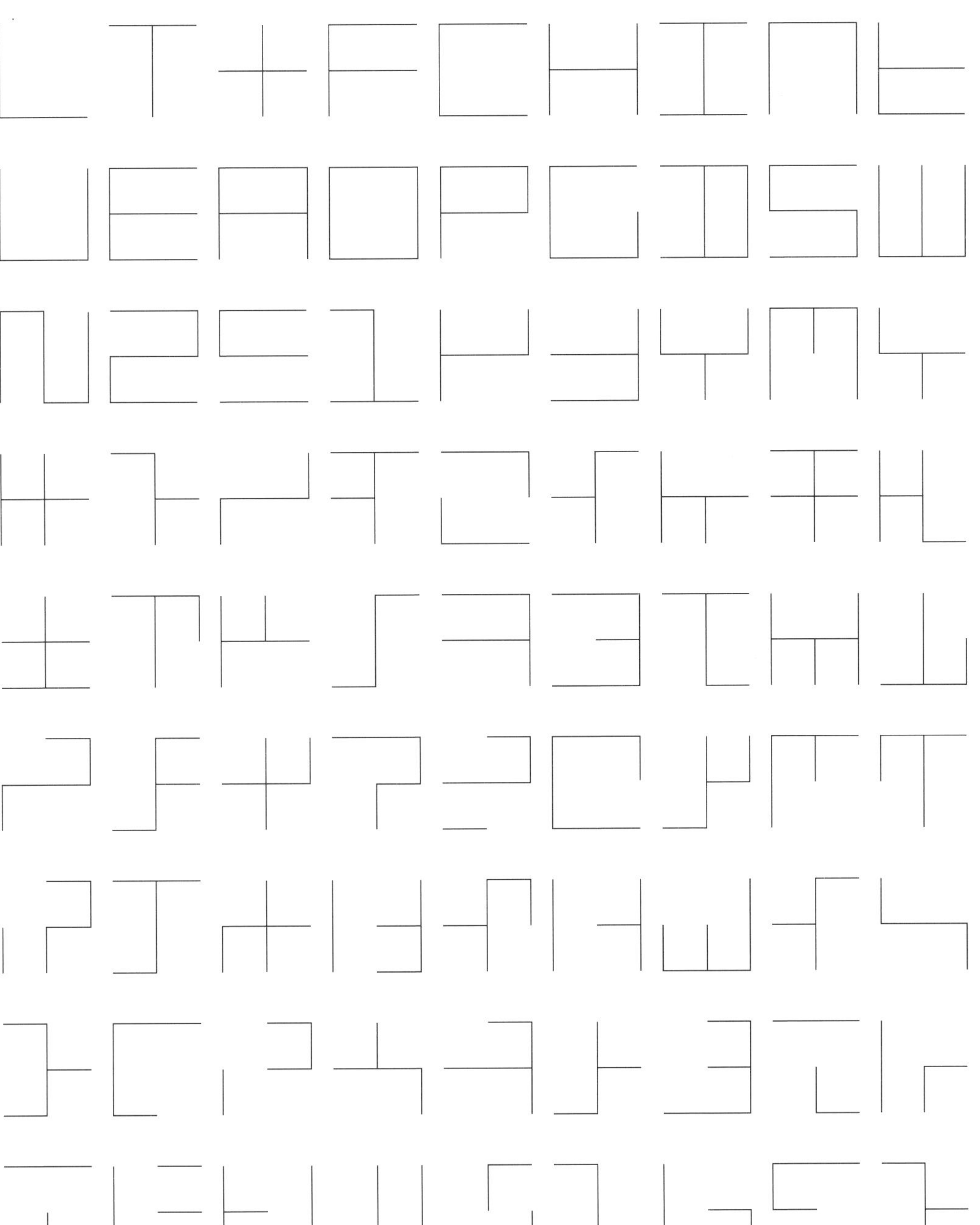

The formative stages of letters. Elementary letter-forms and signs composed of vertical and horizontal strokes. The compositions are angular.

Which two of these 81 forms are equivalent?

How many different signs are possible using only vertical and horizontal strokes?

Common stroke combinations are vertical and horizontal, vertical and slanted, vertical and curvilinear, horizontal and slanted, horizontal and curvilinear, and slanted left and slanted right.

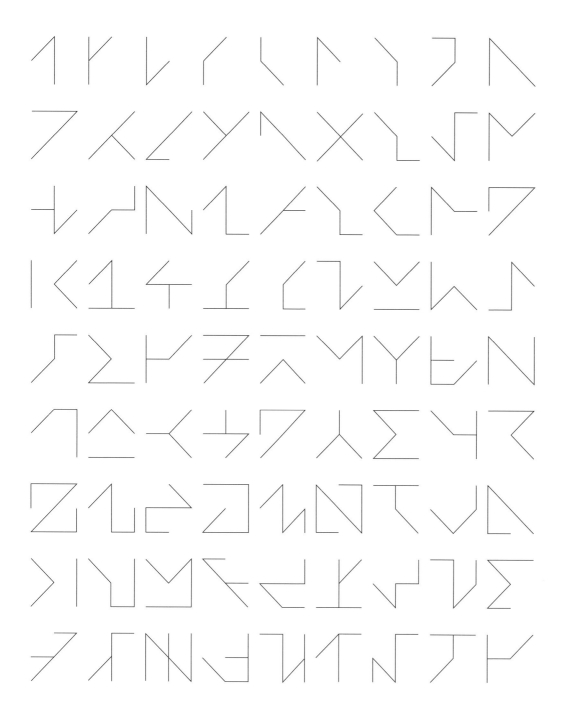

Elementary letterforms and signs composed of vertical, horizontal and slanted strokes. The composition's angularity is increasingly diverse.

Of these 81 forms, two are congruent. Which ones?

How many different signs are possible using only vertical, horizontal, and slanted strokes?

Elementary letterforms and signs composed of vertical, horizontal, slanted and curvilinear strokes. The curvilinear stroke adds a new dynamic to the previously angular compositions. Even though the individual forms are abstract, the forms begin to suggest a typographic composition.

Which two of these 81 forms are the same?

How many different forms are possible using all of the stroke types?

To become familiar with the structure of letters, studies of the elementary forms are essential. The experience and insight gained from these studies will later support the design of logotypes and symbols.

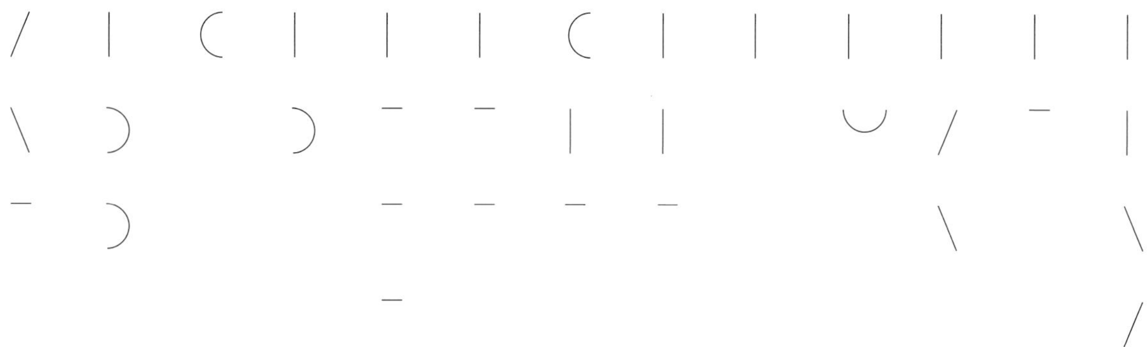

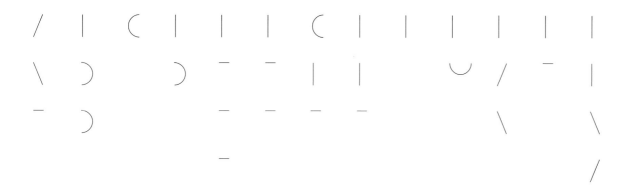

A B C D E F G H I J K L M

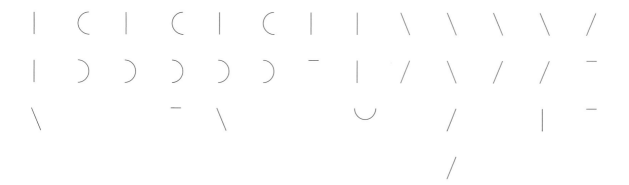

N O P Q R S T U V W X Y Z

Stroke configurations

Each upper and lower case letter consists of a particular set of strokes. The type of strokes and their combination makes each letter unique and provides each letter with its meaning. Composed of one horizontal and two slanted strokes, the letterform A is distinct from a W, which consists of four slanted strokes.

Lower case letterforms differ from each other more than uppercase letters, making them easier to distinguish. Lower case letters are also less affected by simplifications and reductions of form than upper case letters are.

a b c d e f g h i j k l m

n o p q r s t u v w x y z

Survey of strokes in upper and lower case letters. Some letters, such as K, use the same stroke types in upper and lowercase form, while other letters, like A, differ by several strokes.

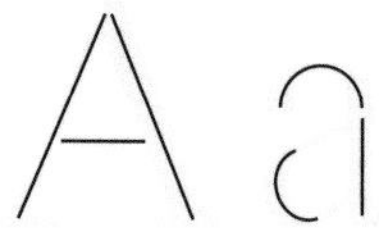

Each letter of the alphabet is designed around a skeleton structure that varies only minimally from typeface to typeface.

The combined topology of Times Roman, Rockwell, and Univers.

Which fonts are exceptions to this thesis?

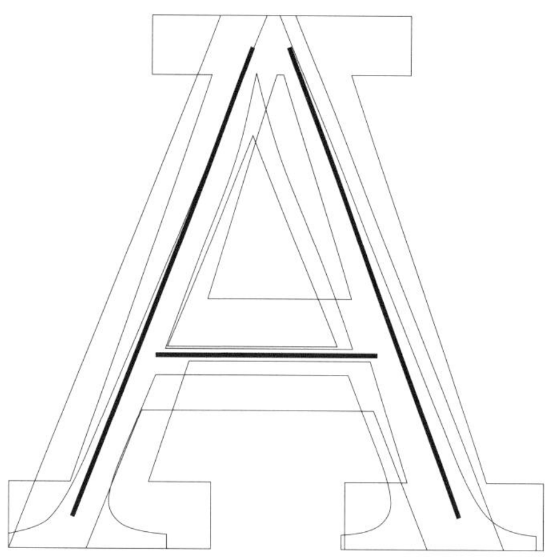

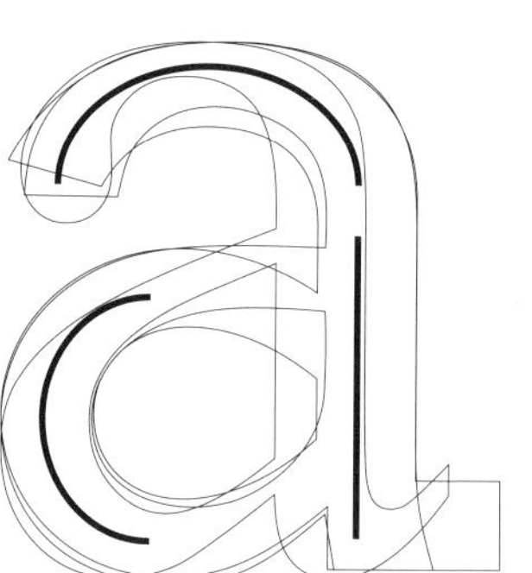

Variation of letterform

The basic structure of each letter is established and varies only minimally from one typeface to another. A letter's structure and function intertwine; to function, the letter's structure must conform to widely accepted norms established over many centuries. The letter's final form depends on details that are subservient to structure.

Each letter derives its final form from variables such as the weight and modulation of strokes, and the absence or presence of serifs. These variables are conducive to infinite variations, as evidenced by the vast number of typefaces available today. Uncommon or extravagant details can distract from the letter's essential form, rendering it primarily decorative.

Through different expressions of final form, a letterform can evoke different emotions. The form may be static or dynamic, plain or ornate, light or heavy. For the typographic designer to meet functional requirements and to achieve the aesthetic and psychological effects of typography, a deep appreciation of all variations of letterform is essential.

A a	A a	A a
A a	A a	A a
A a	A a	A a
A a	A a	A a
A a	A a	A a
A a	A a	A a

Upper case and lower case form variations.

Column one
Akzidenz-Grotesk extended
Univers 59
Grotesque MT black
Verdana italic
Gill Sans
Imago medium italic

Column two
Meta
Courier
Boton
Rockwell bold
Palatino
Baskerville

Column three
Bodoni bold
Times Roman
Bembo
Caslon 540
Centennial bold
Goudy Old Style

Although the structure is the same, the heavy strokes and slab serifs of Rockwell make it feel much sturdier than the more refined Caslon 540.

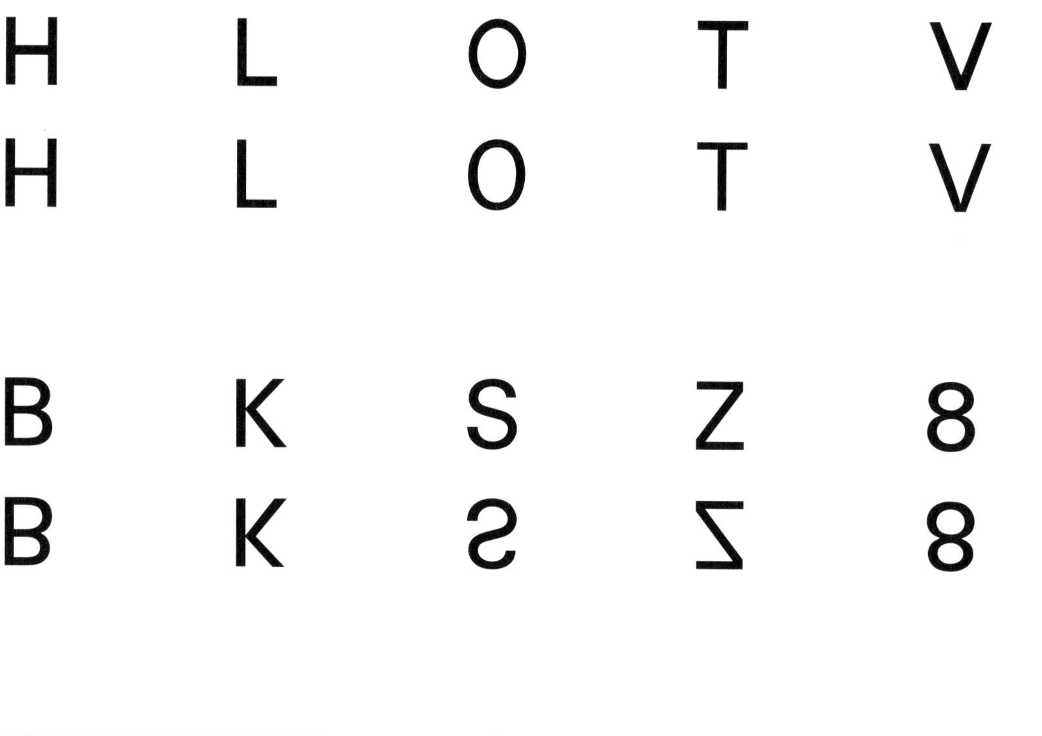

Compared to Univers 55 (bottom), letterforms with a uniform stroke weight appear crude.

Letterforms rotated 180 degrees. To be optically correct, letterforms with horizontal symmetry are actually smaller on top than on the bottom.

Letterforms with uniform, geometrically determined horizontal centerlines appear disproportioned compared to letterforms whose horizontal centerlines are optically determined (bottom).

Letterforms from Futura, a geometric typeface designed by Paul Renner in 1927.

Microaesthetics of form

Each letterform is a highly sophisticated, dynamic element. To appear optically correct, all letterforms depend on optical adjustments and sophisticated microaesthetic detailing. Study of classical typefaces such as Bembo, Garamond, Bodoni, Akzidenz-Grotesk, Futura, and Univers sharpens the sense for the universal qualities inherent in good letterforms.

The following general principles apply to the design of letterforms. To optically align, curves should slightly exceed the base- and x-line. To appear centered, the horizontal centerline should be above the geometric and mathematical horizontal line. To appear equal, vertical strokes must be heavier than horizontal strokes. To appear optically correct, curvilinear strokes should taper at the top and bottom. To avoid buildup of dark spots, slanted intersecting strokes should taper.

Letterforms constructed strictly using the compass, ruler, and French curve appear rigid and static. A good letterform is neither constructed nor measured, nor can it be intellectually analyzed. It is the designer's experience, trained eye and sense of form that shape the optimal letterform.

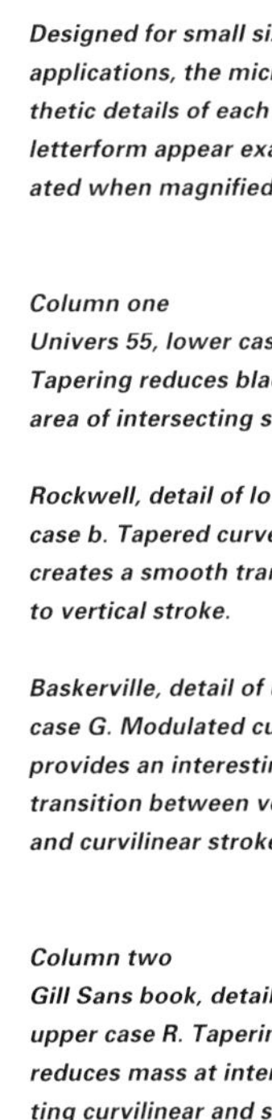

Designed for small size applications, the microaesthetic details of each letterform appear exaggerated when magnified.

Column one
Univers 55, lower case x. Tapering reduces black area of intersecting strokes.

Rockwell, detail of lower case b. Tapered curve creates a smooth transition to vertical stroke.

Baskerville, detail of upper case G. Modulated curve provides an interesting transition between vertical and curvilinear strokes.

Column two
Gill Sans book, detail of upper case R. Tapering reduces mass at intersecting curvilinear and slanted strokes.

Caslon italic, detail of lower case k. Highly modulated slanted and curvilinear strokes create the dynamic letterform.

Bodoni italic, lower case f. Extremely tapered transition between slanted stroke and terminal makes the letterform elegant and powerful.

Futura, designed by Paul Renner in 1927, is one of the few successful geometric typefaces based on the circle, square, and triangle. However, to be optically correct, the intersecting and curvilinear strokes taper and the verticals are slightly heavier than the horizontals.

The universe of microaesthetic details makes letterforms a rich source of inspiration. The design of a typographic symbol often originates in a letterform that seems appropriate for the given context. Among the many typefaces available, there is always a particular form that captures our attention and inspires a typographic solution.

In developing a typographic symbol, why strive for elaborated, constructed forms when sophisticated elements are readily available?

ABCDEFGHIJKLM
NOPQRSTUVWXYZ
1234567890

Cap height

acemnors
uvwxz

x-height

Letters grouped by height.

bdfhiklt

x-height
plus ascenders

gpqy

x-height
plus descender

j

x-height plus ascender
and descender

AHIMOTUVWXY
ilovwx
80

Symmetric

BCDEFGJKLNPQRSZ
abcdefghjkmnpqrstuyz
12345679

Asymmetric

Letters grouped by form.

Letter identity

Attributes of height, form, stroke configuration, and optical weight define each letter's identity.

The letter's height determines the distribution of its weight. Capital letters and numbers, and lower case letters without ascenders or descenders have an even horizontal weight. Letters with ascenders are top-heavy; letters with descenders are bottom-heavy.

The form determines whether a letter is static or dynamic. Symmetric letters are static; asymmetric letters dynamic.

The letter's optical weight refers to its density – how much the letter will subtract from the background.

The stroke configuration determines the optical quality of a letter. Depending on the dominant strokes, a letter is predominantly angular or curvilinear.

Although each letter is distinct, certain attributes – its height, for instance – are shared with other letters. Letters can be grouped by different attributes, such as letters defined by their x-height or letters defined by their cap line. Organized into groups with a common denominator, the similarities and differences of letters and numbers are easier to comprehend and bring logic to how letters and numbers relate to one another.

Open	Dense
CDEFGHJLOPQT UVYZ bcdghmnopqruvyz 12370	ABIKMNRSWX aefjlkstwx 45689

Letters grouped by optical weight.

Vertical horizontal	Vertical horizontal slanted	Vertical horizontal curvilinear	Curvilinear
EFHILT fjlt	AKMN VWXYZ kvwxyz 147	BDGPU bdeghm npqru 25	COQS cos 36890

Letters grouped by predominant stroke.

What other criteria can be used to group letters?

A knowledge and appreciation of letterforms and their individual quirks and assets is essential to typography. The more a designer knows about each letterform and how its parts fit together, the less inhibited he will be in working with type.

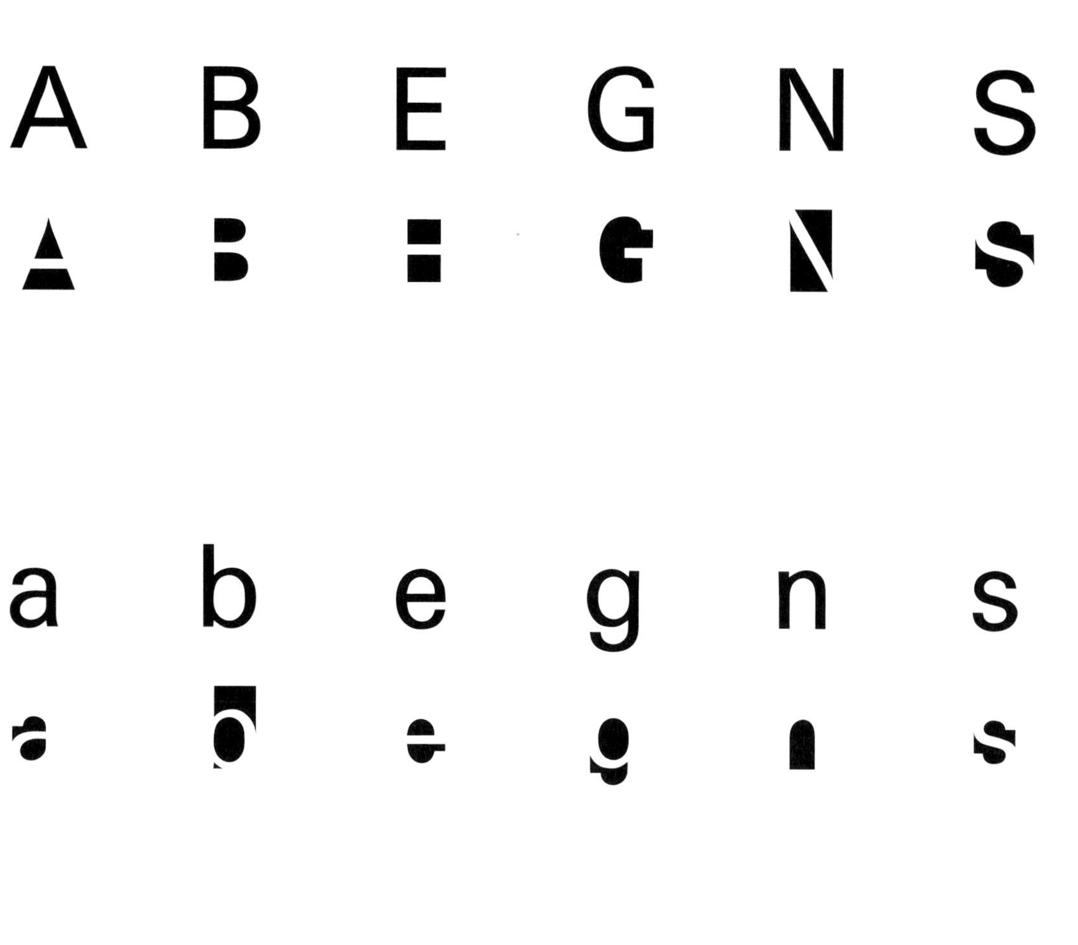

The counterforms of letters create additional typographic forms and expand the possibilities for design.

The counterforms between letters are a rich source of new typographic signs.

Which letterforms create the most interesting counterforms between them?

The counterform of letters

Every letterform consists of solids and voids, the printed positive and the blank negative. The negative form, or counterform, is as much a part of the letter as the positive form. Without a counterform the letter does not exist.

Form and counterform are interdependent, each integral to the letter's design. The counterform is not simply the reversal of form: it is a new entity, the part of the background that emerges through interaction with the foreground. In a good letterform there is an equilibrium between form and counterform. Changing a letter's form inevitably requires an adjustment of the counterform.

When letterforms are combined, new counterforms emerge between them, which dramatically increases the vocabulary of typographic forms.

Reversed out of a black background, the counterform of a letter implies a third dimension. It appears as a figure in a window, and magnifies the style and internal rhythm of a letter.

The interplay between form and counterform is the most fundamental aspect of typography, or any other type of design. In architecture, for instance, the in-between space is as much part of the design as the walls.

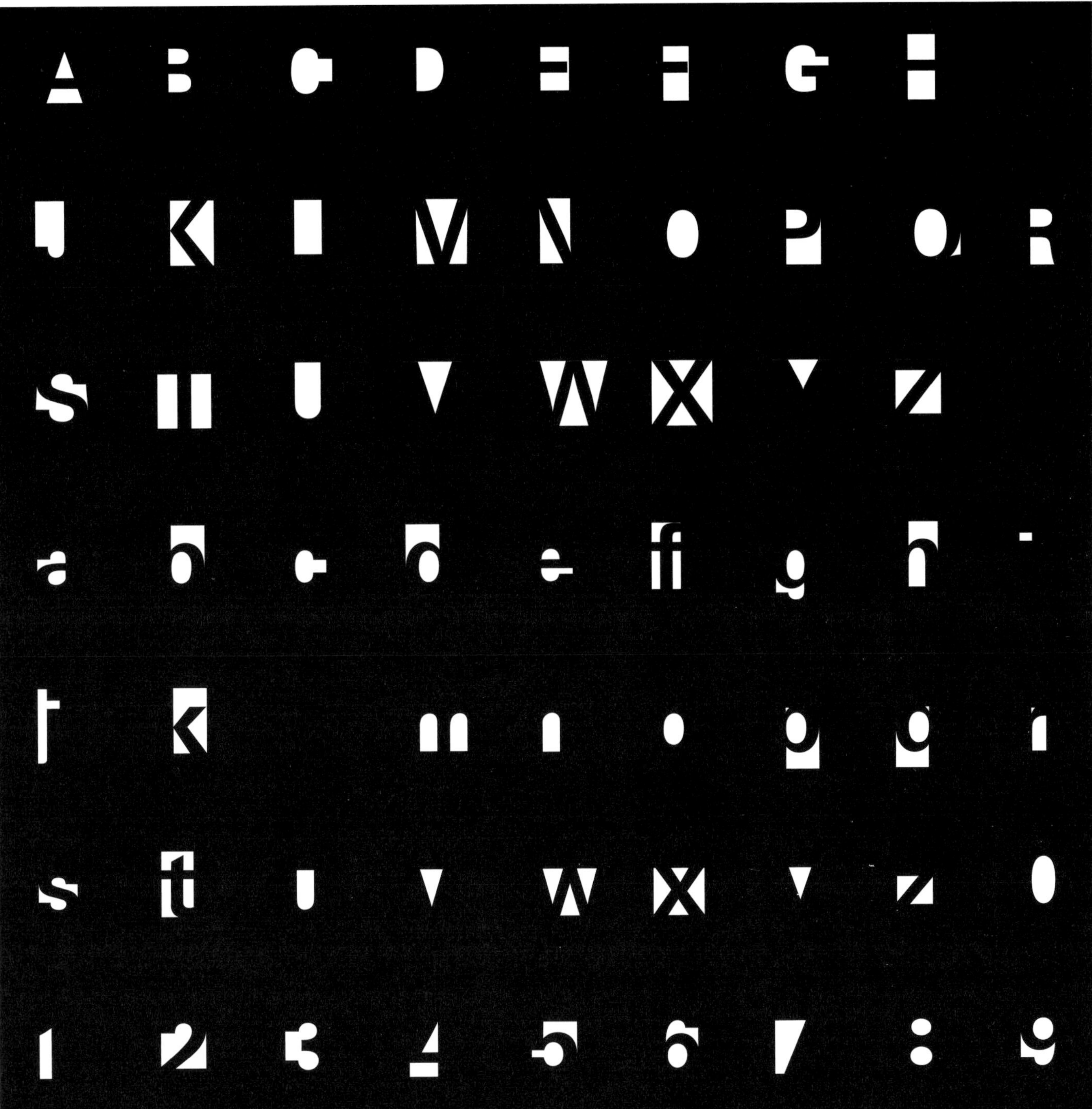

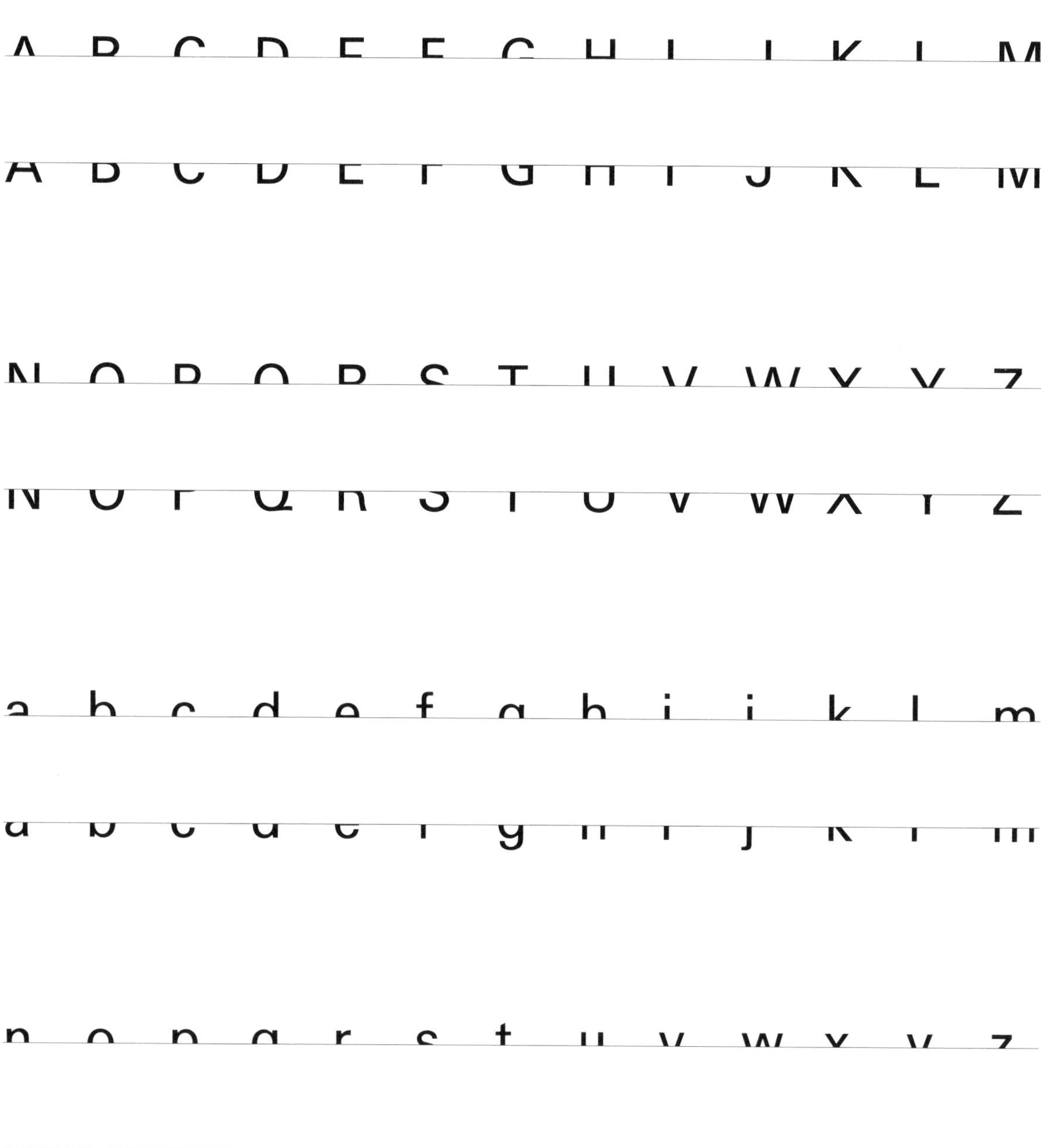

Partial letterforms

When parts of a letterform are missing, the eye completes the form from memory. A partial letterform may be visually intriguing, but its legibility is drastically reduced. When half the letter is obscured either horizontally or vertically, the letter becomes ambiguous. Depending on which part of the form is visible, a letter may retain its identity to some degree.

The upper section, articulated by the x-line and ascender line, carries the primary microaesthetic information defining the letter's identity. The visual cues inherent in the upper section are sufficient to identify most letters.

The lower section, articulated by the baseline and descender line, carries secondary, less familiar information with fewer visual cues to help letter recognition.

When a symmetrical letterform is divided in half vertically, the microaesthetic information of both sections is equal. The visual cues needed to recognize the letters are similar in both halves.

When an asymmetric letterform is divided in half vertically, the optical information in the right section tends to vary more than in the left section. The recognition factor of both sections is about equal.

An important microaesthetic detail of the left section is the letter's optical alignment line; that is, whether a letter is optically flush or not. A letter distinguished by a clear left alignment appears more anchored and stable, and more strongly relates to columns and photographs.

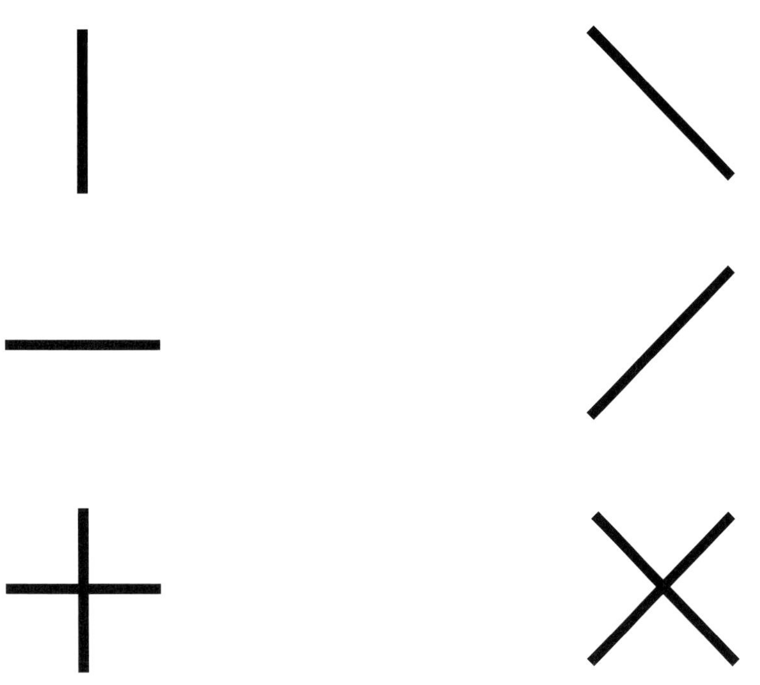

The plus sign consists of a horizontal and a vertical stroke.

Rotated 45 degrees, the plus sign transforms into a multiplication sign composed of two slanted strokes.

In each sequence, an additional step leads to a letterform.

Discovering new forms

Analyzing a letter's internal structure and microaesthetic details is a prerequisite for discovering new forms. Of course, analysis alone is not sufficient to produce anything new; it also requires imagination, creativity and judgment.

Being familiar with the microaesthetic details removes the preconceptions we might have towards certain letterforms. Dissected into their basic components, letterforms yield their complexity; their parts become starting points for exploring new forms. Approached on the microaesthetic level, each letter challenges the imagination and invites pushing the boundaries, leading to new expressions.

A letter is not necessarily the form we are used to seeing, but an element with surprising possibilities for changes and reinterpretation.

Through imagination, rotating, mirroring, and combining, letters and numbers become substitutes for other forms.

Where are the limits to substituting letterforms?

Transforming an A into a new letterform in three steps by different means.

What other transformations of the letter A are possible?

How does the letter A in a serif typeface transform?

How could each of the five sequences continue?

Transformation of letters

Thorough knowledge of form is essential to finding a visual connection between two letters. Close analysis often reveals contact points that are not apparent by cursory examination. For example, letters with slanted and curvilinear intersecting strokes such as A, R, or W are more inspiring and a better source for discovery and development than simple letters like O, I, and L.

An ornate letterform does not necessarily yield more interesting forms. In experimenting with a serif typeface, new forms are obscured by sometimes fussy microaesthetic details.

Letters and numbers offer many possibilities for creative interpretation; with small changes, a letterform transforms into an interesting new sign. The design of a typographic symbol starts with this type of exploration.

Creating new signs by cutting and shifting.

What other means can be used to create new signs?

Are letterforms more conducive to literal or abstract signs?

Discovering new signs

A particular letterform often provides cues for the design of a symbol or logotype. The design development of a visual identity, however, starts not with a letterform but with a clear conceptual idea that meets the project's objective. Letterforms in most instances are part of an established name that cannot be changed. This requires the designer to investigate a letterform from all angles and to discover any idiosyncrasies that may lead to an appropriate concept.

Once the concept is defined, letterforms and letterform transformations can supply the inspiration for exploring new symbols. Developing a symbol with typographic materials progresses through many stages, ending with optical refinements at the microaesthetic level.

Page 34. Development of a symbol for a gasoline distributor, whose name begins with M. The modified capital M suggests a directional traffic sign.

Page 35. Development of a symbol for an executive search firm, whose name begins with C. The lower case c overlapping the two squares suggests connecting two parties.

Development of a symbol for Arrowhead Educational Publishers.
The capital A transforms into an arrowhead.

a

Development of a symbol for an Internet consulting firm whose name begins with a. The section of a Bodoni bold lower case a suggests a path and the sun.

1973

Anspach
Grossman
Portugal
Inc.

1968
Glückwünsche zum Jahreswechsel

Willi Kunz
Eierbrechtstrasse 47
8053 Zürich

Season's greetings card.
Conceptual idea:
show the transition from one year to the next by transforming the numbers 2 and 3.

Season's greetings card.
Conceptual idea:
emphasize the emerging year by transforming the number 8.

Project
Gamma

Project
Gamma

Project
Gamma
Now a closer look

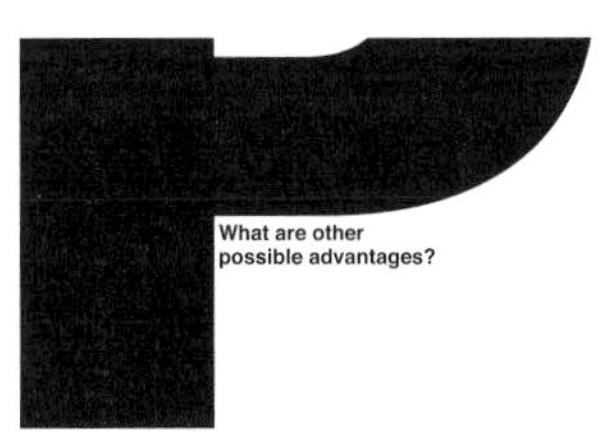
What are other
possible advantages?

How much capital
is required for the project?
What is
the proposal?

What is the
projected volume?

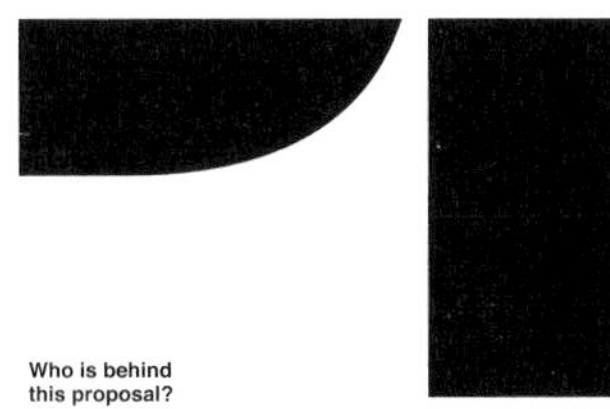
Who is behind
this proposal?

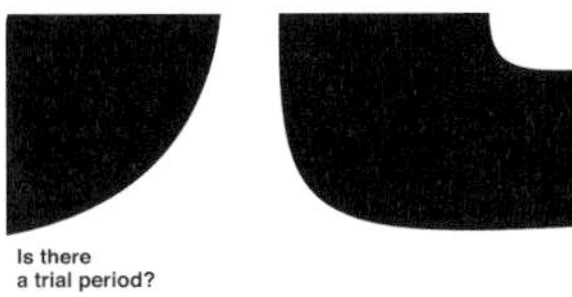
Is there
a trial period?

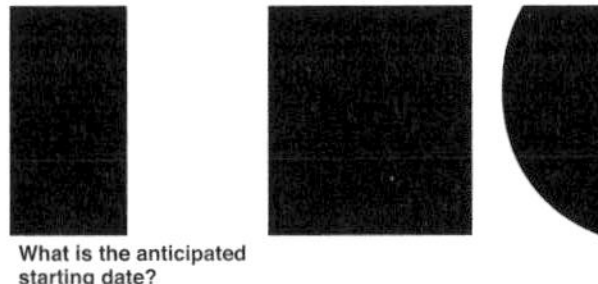
What is the anticipated
starting date?

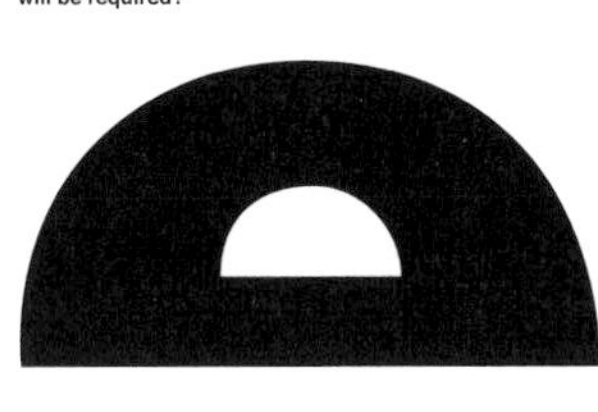
How many ships
will be required?

What are the risks?

Why should you
consider this project?

When will the
ships be provided?

How will the
ships be provided?

What is needed
from Atlantic Richfield?

Is there an initial fee?

What is the competition?

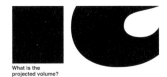

*Question slides for
a sales presentation.
Conceptual idea:
relate all questions to
micro sections of
the title's letterforms.*

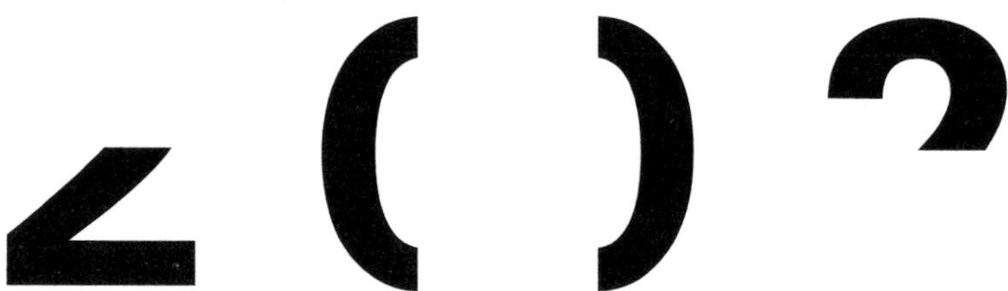

2002 do more with less

Season's greetings card. Conceptual idea: express do more with less *with a minimum of typographic elements.*

Symbol for a gasoline distributor, whose name begins with K. The modified capital K suggests merging of two roads. Related to the studies on page 33.

Tapestry design, 40 x 60 in.
Conceptual idea:
suggest prehistoric signs
from Mexican culture with
typographic forms.
Related to the composition
studies on pages 13, 14,
and 15.

abcdefghijklmnopqrstuvwxyz 1

a r t 2

art 3

The formative stages of a word.
Letters as
1 alphabetical signs,
2 indexical signs,
3 grammatical signs.

---

a

art

part

apart

a part

Permutation of a word by adding letters and space.

A word, and its meaning, is determined by the particular letters it contains and their sequence.

The formation of a word

When letters are combined into words, they change from being indexical signs without specific meaning into grammatical signs that contribute visually to the semantics of the word.

The sequence of letters determines the meaning and form of a word. For instance, four letters combine in twenty-four different ways, but only one combination may yield a specific meaning with a distinct form. Arranged in a different sequence the same letters may yield another meaning with a different form. The sequence of letters is determined by orthography and the syntax structure of language and grammar, which are the basis for all typographic communication.

Combined with other letters to form a syllable or a word, the individual letter's identity becomes secondary. The larger the number of letters, or the more diverse their character, the more each letter's identity is weakened.

part	left	pool	verse
trap	felt	loop	serve

Two words may consist of the same letters, but their meaning will be different depending on the sequence of the letters.

PAGE		SYNTAX	
page		syntax	
Page		Syntax	
ORBIT		QUALITY	
orbit		quality	
Orbit		Quality	

The shape of a word is determined by the form, number, and sequence of its letters.

Word shape

The eye of the sophisticated reader focuses on syllables or complete word shapes, not on individual letters. The shape of a familiar, frequently used word that is part of our visual memory is comprehended more quickly than an unfamiliar word. Because it is integral to both the legibility and readability of type, the shape of a word is crucial.

The designer can manipulate word shape to some extent. Generally, words are set in lower case letters. The initial letter of a word starting a sentence is set in upper case. Variations of x-height, ascenders, and descenders provide lower case words with a unique, lively shape.

A word set in upper case letters is uniformly rectangular. The lack of x-height variations, ascenders, and descenders makes a word set in all upper case letters more difficult to read. The problems of legibility compound when several words or a larger text are set in all upper case letters. In addition, a word set in upper case requires considerably more horizontal space than the same word set in all lower case.

FLEET	FLEET	*A word's rhythm is created by the predominant strokes of its letterforms.*
WAVY	\/\/\/\/	
access	oooooo	
letter	lollol	
novel	llovol	

---

type	type	*Decomposed into syllables, a word's optical syntax and rhythm are pronounced. The syllables articulate the word's structure and tie its expression to its meaning. For instance, vocabulary divided into syllables alludes to its presentation in a dictionary.*
inform	in|form	
syllable	syl|la|ble	
vocabulary	vo|cab|u|lary	
typographical	ty|po|graph|i|cal	

Word rhythm

Each word has an optical rhythm created by the combination of vertical, horizontal, slanted, and curvilinear strokes of its individual letters. The rhythm of a word composed of angular letterforms is dramatically different from one composed of curvilinear letters. The rhythm of a word set in all upper case is different from a word set in all lower case.

The type of composition chosen may enhance the semantics of a word. For instance, the word *peak* set in lower case has little optical elevation – it appears squat with a subtle rhythm. Set in upper case, PEAK has a strong rhythm; the capital A reinforces the semantics of the word and could become the focal point of a design.

The grammatical components of a word are syllables, consisting of one or more letters. Syllables are guides to hyphenation and pronunciation. The syllables of a word create a subliminal reading rhythm.

Syllables stress the individual parts of a word and may be used to enhance its meaning. Divided into syllables, a uniform word like *information* becomes optically active, as if stressing individual pieces of information. In working with text, a strong command over the

information

i n f o r m a t i o n

in for ma tion

i n f o r mation

in f o r m a tion

in forma t i o n

in f o r m a tion

---

i n f o r m a t i o n

---

i n f o r m a t i o n

Normal spacing. The word appears as a unit.

Increased spacing makes individual letters more pronounced.

Varied spacing for contrast between letters and syllables.

Progressive spacing, increasing and decreasing, for optical effect.

syllables of words is essential. Good line breaks often depend on dividing a word into syllables in ways other than those provided automatically by layout programs.

Letterspace significantly affects the formation of a word. Slight changes in letterspace make a big difference in how a word is perceived.

Letterspace is flexible. It ranges from the normal spacing of text to extremely open spacing that emphasizes individual letterforms or syllables. For optical effect, and to stress the rhythm of a word, spacing can be progressive, either increasing or decreasing.

context

1

Normal letterspace optically balances the counterforms of lower case letters.
1 Optimum letterspace.
2 Letterspace is too open.
3 Letterspace is too tight.

context

2

context

3

context

1

Typefaces with small counterforms require less letterspace than typefaces with large counterforms.
1 Optimum letterspace.
2 Letterspace is too open.
3 Letterspace is too tight.

context

2

context

3

The counterforms of lower case letters determine optimum letterspace. Typefaces with small counterforms require less space between letters than those with large counterforms. For optimum legibility, letterspace should be neither too tight nor too open. The goal is to make the space between letters appear even.

The correct letter spacing ultimately determines how a word is perceived. A typographic designer may need to exercise judgment in making necessary adjustments to the letter combinations in a word. Except for special effect, words in larger bodies of text should not be individually letterspaced. For a flawless appearance, a word set in capital letters requires additional attention to the individual spacing between letters.

tunnel

bo ok

pi one er

eye

l one ly

look

LEVEL

TOP

Semantics are enhanced by a word's optical features.

Column one
The double n alludes to a tunnel, the letters t and l to its beginning and end.

one *expresses being first, being the pioneer.*

one *expresses being singular, isolated, lonely.*

The horizontal bars of the double E and L allude to different levels.

Column two
The double o symmetry alludes to the double page spread of a book.

The double e alludes to eyes.

The double o alludes to glasses.

The T and P are top heavy.

Can you find other words with strong connections between their form and meaning?

Word expression

The letterforms that make up a word have specific optical features that lend the word additional expressive qualities. Particular letters, for example, enhance or reinforce the semantics of a word. In some instances, the letterforms clearly and directly express the word's meaning.

A short word consisting of a small number of strong letters generally has a stronger expression than a long word with a variety of characters, because the many divergent characters create an ambiguous impression. Discovering the idiosyncrasies of words is stimulating and challenging, and can become the basis for developing a logotype.

Of course, designers do not usually get to choose a word's letters and their sequence; however, the designer may take advantage of situations in which the meaning of a word and its optical expression are complimentary or contradictory.

page

page

page

page

PAGE

p
a
g
e

p a g e

page

e
g
a
p

Word transformation

To articulate meaning and evoke emotions, a word must be able to communicate via different voices. Similar to intonation in spoken language, different voices can be conveyed by changing a word's presentation.

A style change, from regular to open letterspacing for instance, drastically transforms a word. Changes in case, slant, weight, width, size, and direction also affect a word's expression.

Changing the typeface is the most common way of transforming a word. There are many different typefaces, each with its own inherent expression and associations.

The typeface, through its connotations, can either work for or against the meaning of a word. Through its association with a particular typeface, a word evokes an emotional response.

Changing the reading orientation from horizontal to vertical dramatically changes the visual expression of a word. By drawing a reader's attention, the word becomes a strong contrasting element.

page

page

page

page

page

page

page

page

page

Page 48. Column one

normal setting

Transformation through:
half tone screen
increased letterspace

Column two

Transformation through:
decreased letterspace
upper case setting
italic setting

Column three

Transformation through:
changing direction
vertical setting
diagonal setting

Page 49. Column one

Transformation through:
light font
bold font
condensed font

Column two

Transformation through:
expanded font
reduced size
enlarged size

Column three

Transformation through:
serif typeface
script typeface
decorative typeface

Typogram
900 Broadway
New York, NY10003
212 505 1640

Cover for a brochure on Univers photo typesetting. The decreasing size of the seven letters in relation to the ruler suggests composing type to specified sizes.

TV CONTACT

Xing

TV Contact, logotype for a TV newsletter. The rhythm of gradually closing letterspaces suggests the semantics of contact.

01. The design for a season's greetings card takes advantage of the negative space between 0 and 1.

Xing, logotype for a furniture designer. The cross bars of the X and the changing type size suggest an assembly process.

Twenty-three miles from Agra

Twenty-three miles from Agra in India, with its fabled Taj Mahal

Twenty-three miles from Agra in India, with its fabled Taj Mahal

Twenty-three miles from Agra in India, with its fabled Taj Mahal

Length, weight and direction define the typographical line.

Twenty-three miles from Agra in India, with its fabled Taj Mahal

Word length and spacing create the line's rhythm.

Formation of text

The typographic line

The typographic line consists of one or more words. The line is defined by its length, weight, and direction. The number of words and their size determines the line length. The type style and the size of words determine the line weight. Reading conventions establish the horizontal line direction as primary; for contrast, the designer introduces the vertical or angular line.

Each line has a particular shape. The consistent height of capital letters creates a uniform, rectangular line. The ascenders and descenders of lower case letters provide a more differentiated line.

Line rhythm is created by the interplay between uniform word spacing and varying word lengths. Open word spacing accentuates the line rhythm. However, it fragments the line and slows down reading. Generally, a line looks best with tight, optically unobtrusive word spaces. The width of the lower case i is optimal.

TWENTY-THREE MILES FROM AGRA IN INDIA, WITH ITS FABLED TAJ MAHAL, LIES FATEPUR SIKRI, A DREAM CITY BUILT IN SANDSTONE THE COLORS OF THE DYING SUNSET. ONE APPROACHES FATEPUR SIKRI IN SILENCE, FOR IT HAS BEEN DESERTED FOR OVER TWO HUNDRED YEARS, BUT IMMEDIATELY

Text set in all capital letters and to a wide measure is among the most offensive typographic practices. Only a determined reader will decipher text set in this way.

A line consisting of more than 100 characters is difficult and tiring to read.

The optimal line consists of approximately ten medium-length words.

Short lines consisting of less than four words appear fragmented.

Twenty-three miles from Agra in India, with its fabled Taj Mahal, lies Fatepur Sikri, a dream city built in sand stone the colors of the dying sunset. One approaches Fatepur Sikri in silence, for it has been deserted for over two hundred years, but immediately on entering the core of the city, the Mahal-i-Khas, the heart is uplifted, the eye entranced. One experiences a rare sensation of freedom and repose, an invitation to step forward buoyantly and, at the same time, to loiter luxuriously. Wherever the eye turns the view is held, but at every step it changes. A seemingly solid background wall of stone is later perceived as a transparent screen. But nowhere is there a fixed center: nowhere a point from which the observer can dominate the whole. Equally nowhere does he stand conspicuously removed from the center, a spectator in the wings. From the moment he steps within this urban core he becomes an intimate part of the scene, which does not impose itself upon him, but discloses

Twenty-three miles from Agra in India, with its fabled Taj Mahal, lies Fatepur Sikri, a dream city built in sandstone the colors of the dying sun-set. One approaches Fatepur Sikri in silence, for it has been deserted for over two hundred years, but immediately on entering the core of the city, the Mahal-i-Khas, the heart is uplifted, the eye entranced. One experiences a rare sensation of freedom and repose, an invitation to step forward

Twenty-three miles from Agra in India, with its fabled Taj Mahal, lies Fatepur Sikri, a dream city built in sand-stone the colors of the dying sunset. One approaches Fatepur

---

Line length

A long line stretching across the page is difficult to read. For legibility, a long line should be subdivided into a series of short lines. The length should be such that the eye easily follows the lines without tiring or stalling when moving from one line to the next. The other extreme – very short lines requiring the eye to frequently change direction – should also be avoided.

The optimal line contains between four and ten average length words. The line length is linked to the type size and number of words: the larger the type size and the number of words, the longer the line.

Alignment

The most common ways to align text are flush left, ragged right; flush right, ragged left; centered (middle axis); free form; and justified.

The flush left, ragged right composition is generally preferred. The contrast between the vertical alignment on the left and the ragged edge on the right provides visual interest to the text. Vertically aligned on the left, the sequence of lines is easy for the eye to follow .

The flush left ragged right composition starts with a short line and then alternates between long and short lines. The composition has an animated but even ragged edge.

Twenty-three miles from Agra in India, with its fabled Taj Mahal, lies Fatepur Sikri, a dream city built in sandstone the colors of the dying sunset. One approaches Fatepur Sikri in silence, for it has been deserted for over two hundred years, but immediately on entering the core

Twenty-three miles from Agra in India, with its fabled Taj Mahal, lies Fatepur Sikri, a dream city built in sandstone the colors of the dying sunset. One approaches Fatepur Sikri in silence, for it has been deserted for over two hundred years, but immediately on entering the core

Twenty-three miles from Agra in India,
with its fabled Taj Mahal,
lies Fatepur Sikri, a dream city built in sandstone
the colors of the dying sunset.
One approaches Fatepur Sikri in silence,
for it has been deserted

Twenty-three miles from Agra in India,
with its fabled Taj Mahal,
lies Fatepur Sikri, a dream city
built in sandstone the colors of the dying sunset.
One approaches Fatepur Sikri in silence,
for it has been deserted for over two

Twenty-three miles
from Agra in India,
with its fabled Taj Mahal,
lies Fatepur Sikri,
a dream city
built in sandstone

Twenty-three
miles
from
Agra
in
India,
with
its
fabled
Taj
Mahal
lies
Fatepur
Sikri,
a
dream
city
built
in
sandstone

Column one
Justified text.
Flush right text.
Centered text.
Free form text.

Column two
Line breaks according to syntax.

Single word per line.

In justified text, the forced alignment on the right creates word spaces of varying widths, breaking up the line rhythm and marring the text with a spotty, uneven texture. Uniform word space is more important to text than even line length. Text consisting of alternately jammed and loosely spaced lines is disturbing to the eye.

Lacking a clear left alignment, lines composed flush right, centered, or free form are difficult to read. These types of composition are unsuited for text. They also lack the intellectual rigor and tension necessary for good typographic design.

A good flush left, ragged right or justified composition can only be achieved by hyphenating words. Aesthetic considerations, logic, and grammar determine when and where words are hyphenated. Just as a single word should not be awkwardly broken, words or numbers that function as a unit such as New York, Le Corbusier, or 200 million should not be separated. Short words and syllables should not be left dangling at the end of a line.

Dividing the lines according to the syntax structure of the text creates extremely fluctuating line lengths that are tiresome to read, requiring additional mental effort.

Twenty-three miles from Agra in India, with its fabled Taj Mahal, lies Fatepur Sikri, a dream city built in sandstone the colors of the dying sunset.

One approaches Fatepur Sikri in silence, for it has been deserted for over two hundred years, but immediately on entering the core of the city, the Mahal-i-Khas, the heart is uplifted, the eye entranced. One experiences a rare sensation of freedom and repose, an invitation to step forward buoyantly and, at the same time, to loiter luxuriously. Wherever the eye turns the view is held, but at every step it changes.

A seemingly solid background wall of stone is later perceived as a transparent screen. But nowhere is there a fixed center: nowhere a point from which the observer can dominate the whole. Equally nowhere does he stand conspicuously removed from the center, a spectator in the wings. From the moment he steps within this urban core he becomes an intimate part of the scene, which does not impose

Twenty-three miles from Agra in India, with its fabled Taj Mahal, lies Fatepur Sikri, a dream city built in sandstone the colors of the dying sunset.

One approaches Fatepur Sikri in silence, for it has been deserted for over two hundred years, but immediately on entering the core of the city, the Mahal-i-Khas, the heart is uplifted, the eye entranced. One experiences a rare sensation of freedom and repose, an invitation to step forward buoyantly and, at the same time, to loiter luxuriously. Wherever the eye turns the view is held, but at every step it changes.

A seemingly solid background wall of stone is later perceived as a transparent screen. But nowhere is there a fixed center: nowhere a point from which the observer can dominate the whole. Equally nowhere does he stand conspicuously removed from the center, a spectator in the wings. From the moment he steps within this

Column one
Paragraph separation by indented line.

Paragraph separation by extended line.

Column two
Paragraph separation by line space.

Paragraph separation by remaining white space of last line.

Twenty-three miles from Agra in India, with its fabled Taj Mahal, lies Fatepur Sikri, a dream city built in sandstone the colors of the dying sunset.

One approaches Fatepur Sikri in silence, for it has been deserted for over two hundred years, but immediately on entering the core of the city, the Mahal-i-Khas, the heart is uplifted, the eye entranced. One experiences a rare sensation of freedom and repose, an invitation to step forward buoyantly and, at the same time, to loiter luxuriously. Wherever the eye turns the view is held, but at every step it changes.

A seemingly solid background wall of stone is later perceived as a transparent screen. But nowhere is there a fixed center: nowhere a point from which the observer can dominate the whole. Equally nowhere does he stand conspicuously removed from the center, a spectator in the wings. From the moment

Twenty-three miles from Agra in India, with its fabled Taj Mahal, lies Fatepur Sikri, a dream city built in sandstone the colors of the dying sunset.

One approaches Fatepur Sikri in silence, for it has been deserted for over two hundred years, but immediately on entering the core of the city, the Mahal-i-Khas, the heart is uplifted, the eye entranced. One experiences a rare sensation of freedom and repose, an invitation to step forward buoyantly and, at the same time, to loiter luxuriously. Wherever the eye turns the view is held, but at every step it changes.

A seemingly solid background wall of stone is later perceived as a transparent screen. But nowhere is there a fixed center: nowhere a point from which the observer can dominate the whole. Equally nowhere does he stand conspicuously removed from the center, a spectator in the wings. From the moment he steps within this urban core he becomes an intimate part of the scene,

---

Paragraphs

Paragraphs are essential for readability. By subdividing the text into thought units, paragraphs provide typographic structure. They introduce a rhythm and make the text inviting to the reader.

The start of a paragraph is highlighted by indenting or extending the first line, or by inserting a line space. The effective paragraph indent is decisive and clear; it is no less than one eighth of the line width. Small indentions of one em space or less create an ambiguous, serrated left-hand edge, especially with short paragraphs. The first paragraph is set without an indent.

Paragraphs marked by an extended first line require a certain length. The extended line should not appear too often, otherwise it makes both the left- and right-hand edge look ragged.

The most explicit way to separate paragraphs is by a full line space. Short paragraphs separated by full line space appear fragmented, however. Spaces of less than one line between paragraphs look ambiguous and disturb the line rhythm.

The remaining white space of a paragraph's last line is not effective in differentiating paragraphs.

Twenty-three miles from Agra in India, with its fabled Taj Mahal, lies Fatepur Sikri, a dream city built in sandstone the colors of the dying sunset. One approaches Fatepur Sikri in silence, for it has been deserted for over two hundred years, but immediately on entering the core of the city, the Mahal-i-Khas, the

Twenty-three miles from Agra in India, with its fabled Taj Mahal, lies Fatepur Sikri, a dream city built in sandstone the colors of the dying sunset. One approaches Fatepur Sikri in silence, for it has been deserted for over two hundred years, but immediately on entering the core of the city, the Mahal-i-Khas, the heart is uplifted, the eye entranced. One experiences a rare sensation of freedom and repose, an invitation to step forward buoyantly and, at the same time, to loiter luxuriously. Wherever the eye turns the view is held, but at every step it changes. A seemingly solid background wall of stone is later perceived as a transparent screen. But nowhere is there a fixed

Twenty-three miles from Agra in India, with its fabled Taj Mahal, lies Fatepur Sikri, a dream city built in sandstone the colors of the dying sunset. One approaches Fatepur Sikri in silence, for it has been deserted for over two hundred years, but immediately on entering the core of the city, the Mahal-i-Khas, the

Twenty-three miles from Agra in India, with its fabled Taj Mahal, lies Fatepur Sikri, a dream city built in sandstone the colors of the dying sunset. One approaches Fatepur Sikri in silence, for it has been deserted for over two hundred years, but immediately on entering the core of the city, the Mahal-i-Khas, the heart is uplifted, the eye entranced. One experiences a rare sensation of freedom and repose, an invitation to step forward buoyantly and, at the same time, to loiter luxuriously. Wherever the eye turns the view is held, but at every step it changes. A seemingly solid background wall of stone is later perceived as a transparent screen. But nowhere is there a fixed

Twenty-three miles from Agra in India, with its fabled Taj Mahal, lies Fatepur Sikri, a dream city built in sandstone the colors of the dying sunset. One approaches Fatepur Sikri in silence, for it has been deserted for over two hundred years, but immediately on entering the core of the city, the Mahal-i-Khas, the

Twenty-three miles from Agra in India, with its fabled Taj Mahal, lies Fatepur Sikri, a dream city built in sandstone the colors of the dying sunset. One approaches Fatepur Sikri in silence, for it has been deserted for over two hundred years, but immediately on entering the core of the city, the Mahal-i-Khas, the heart is uplifted, the eye entranced. One experiences a rare sensation of freedom and repose, an invitation to step forward buoyantly and, at the same time, to loiter luxuriously. Wherever the eye turns the view is held, but at every step it changes. A seemingly solid background wall of stone is later perceived as a transparent screen. But nowhere is there a fixed

Twenty-three miles from Agra in India, with its fabled Taj Mahal, lies Fatepur Sikri, a dream city built in sandstone the colors of the dying sunset. One approaches Fatepur Sikri in silence, for it has been deserted for over two hundred years, but immediately on entering the core of the city, the Mahal-i-Khas, the

Twenty-three miles from Agra in India, with its fabled Taj Mahal, lies Fatepur Sikri, a dream city built in sandstone the colors of the dying sunset. One approaches Fatepur Sikri in silence, for it has been deserted for over two hundred years, but immediately on entering the core of the city, the Mahal-i-Khas, the heart is uplifted, the eye entranced. One experiences a rare sensation of freedom and repose, an invitation to step forward buoyantly and, at the same time, to loiter luxuriously. Wherever the eye turns the view is held, but at every step it changes. A seemingly solid background wall of stone is later perceived as a transparent screen. But nowhere is there a fixed

Text set in 7 pt Univers 55. From top to bottom

Set solid.
Set with 2 point interline space.
Set with 3.5 point interline space.
Set with 7 point interline space.

The narrow text column appears more open than the wide column.

Text becomes difficult to read when set either solid – that is, with the same numeric value applied to both the type size and the interline space – or with too much interline space.

Optical values

The optical quality of text is defined by the texture, or gray value, of the lines. A text that is attractive to the reader, easy to read, and appealing to the eye is distinguished by an engaging texture. Attention to texture, however, should not degrade into frivolous pattern making or be considered as a gray value for aesthetic effect.

Texture derives from the variables of typeface, type size, line length, and interline space. Combined in innumerable ways, these four variables yield a vast range of different textures that are a versatile, subtle element in design with text.

Of the four variables contributing to texture, the most subtle and demanding is the interline space. Without the proper interline space, the quality of the most carefully composed lines is lost. Experimentation with interline space is at the heart of creating the appropriate texture for a design.

Interline space is inextricably linked to line length and the x-height of the typeface used. Composed in the same type size and face, and with the same interline space, a wide column of text appears heavier in texture than a narrow column. To achieve the same texture, the interline

Twenty-three miles from Agra in India, with its fabled Taj Mahal, lies Fatepur Sikri, a dream city built in sandstone the colors of the dying sunset. One approaches Fatepur Sikri in silence, for it has been deserted for over two hundred years, but immediately on entering the core of the city, the Mahal-i-Khas, the heart is uplifted, the eye entranced. One experiences a rare sensation of freedom and repose, an invitation to step forward buoyantly and, at the same time, to loiter luxuriously. Wherever the eye turns the view is held, but at every step it changes. A seemingly solid background wall of stone is later perceived as a transparent screen. But nowhere is there a fixed center: nowhere a point from which the observer can dominate the whole. Equally nowhere does he stand conspicuously removed from the center, a spectator in the

Twenty-three miles from Agra in India, with its fabled Taj Mahal, lies Fatepur Sikri, a dream city built in sandstone the colors of the dying sunset. One approaches Fatepur Sikri in silence, for it has been deserted for over two hundred years, but immediately on entering the core of the city, the Mahal-i-Khas, the heart is uplifted, the eye entranced. One experiences a rare sensation of freedom and repose, an invitation to step forward buoyantly and, at the

Typeface, size, and leading determine the texture of type.

Twenty-three miles from Agra in India, with its fabled Taj Mahal, lies Fatepur Sikri, a dream city built in sand-stone the colors of the dying sunset. One approaches

Twenty-three miles from Agra in India, with its fabled Taj Mahal, lies Fatepur Sikri, a dream city built in sandstone the colors of the dying sunset. One approaches Fatepur Sikri in silence, for it has been deserted for over two hundred years, but immediately on entering the core of the city, the Mahal-i-Khas, the heart is uplifted, the eye entranced. One experiences a rare sensation of freedom and repose, an invitation to step forward buoyantly and, at the same time, to loiter luxuriously. Wherever the eye turns the view is held, but at every step

Twenty-three miles from Agra in India, with its fabled Taj Mahal, lies Fatepur Sikri, a dream city built in sandstone the colors of the dying sunset. One approaches Fatepur Sikri in silence, for it has been deserted for over two hundred years, but immediately on entering the core of the city, the Mahal-i-Khas, the heart is uplifted, the eye entranced. One experiences a rare

Twenty-three miles from Agra in India, with its fabled Taj Mahal, lies Fatepur Sikri, a dream city built in sandstone the colors of the dying sunset. One approaches Fatepur Sikri in silence, for it has been deserted for over two hundred years, but immediately on entering the core of the city, the Mahal-i-Khas, the heart is uplifted, the eye entranced. One experiences a rare sensation of freedom and repose, an invitation to step forward buoyantly and, at the same time, to loiter luxuriously. Wherever the eye turns the view is held, but at every step

Twenty-three miles from Agra in India, with its fabled Taj Mahal, lies Fatepur Sikri, a dream city built in sandstone the colors of the dying sunset. One approaches Fatepur Sikri in silence, for it has been deserted for over two hundred years, but immediately on entering the core of the city, the Mahal-i-Khas, the heart is uplifted, the eye

Twenty-three miles from Agra in India, with its fabled Taj Mahal, lies Fatepur Sikri, a dream city built in sand-stone the colors of the dying sunset. One approaches Fatepur Sikri in silence, for it has been deserted for over two hundred years, but immediately on entering the core of the city, the Mahal-i-Khas, the heart is uplifted, the eye entranced. One experiences a rare sensation of freedom and repose, an invitation to step forward buoyantly and, at the same time, to loiter luxuriously. Wherever the eye turns the view is held, but at every

---

space of the narrow column would have to be decreased. When space is limited, selecting a typeface with a small x-height, which requires less interline space, over a typeface with a large x-height, which requires more, may be crucial.

By changing the interline space, dramatically different textures are obtained from a single typeface composed in a single type size. By changing the type size, the range of textures increases again.

The capacity of interline space as a means for achieving a desired texture still surprises me. A quarter point of interline space, while changing the texture only slightly, can make the difference between an ordinary and a refined design solution. However, in many instances it is the elements of the text, such as the number of capital letters and numerals it contains, that contribute to the texture in an unanticipated way.

A text composed in a single, wide column is unappealing.

Divided into columns, the text becomes inviting. Its quantity appears reduced.

Columns

A text composed in a single, wide column appears forbidding. The reader will spend little time with the text and pass it for something more accessible.

Text presented in two or more columns is structured. Its quantity appears reduced, and the more playful presentation engages the reader. As the number of columns increases, the text becomes more interesting visually.

If the text is presented in an accessible way there is no limit to quantity. Divided into columns the text becomes manageable. The number of columns depends on the type of information to be presented, and on the design objectives.

The index set in a smaller type size requires narrower columns than the text of a book.

The space between columns is related to the interline space of the text. The more open the interline space, the greater the space that is needed between the columns to optically separate them. The space between the columns should appear wider than the interline space of the text.

Arbitrary space between paragraphs has a negative effect on columns; lines do not register across the page, resulting in a sloppy appearance.

Columns of text are placed asymmetrically. A centered column lacks tension with the vertical boundaries of the space.

Columns aligned at the top are easier to navigate than those aligned at the bottom or with shifting alignments.

Column placement

Columns are placed asymmetrically, either related to the left or to the right edge of the space. Centered columns lack tension with the vertical boundaries of the space.

For text, most columns are justified top and bottom, or flush at the top and ragged at the bottom. The level alignment at the top makes it easy for the eye to identify the start of each column.

Less common are columns that are flush at the bottom and ragged at the top, or ragged at the top and at the bottom. Though the irregular alignments look playful, the constantly shifting columns are difficult to navigate.

Text with mixed column widths, based on three and four columns.

What other text layouts with mixed column widths are possible?

Mixed column widths

The nature of a text sometimes invites a departure from uniform column width. A conversation between different persons, for instance, may use different column widths to establish a hierarchy. By assigning a different column width to each person, the text is animated.

It is important, however, that a clear connection between the different parts of the text is maintained and that the eye is not distracted by the different column widths and is unable to follow the content. By working with different column widths, it is easy to get lost in the formal aspects of the design.

In working with mixed column widths, the space is first subdivided into a number of narrow columns. The text is then composed on multiples of these columns. Working with a mixture of different columns challenges the designer. The text must be appropriate for this type of treatment.

World War I did not not affect Japan, but she fought her own victorious war with Russia in 1905 and in 1931 invaded Manchuria. Emperor Meiji died in 1912 and Taisho in 1926.

While modernism and modern architecture with its 'International Style' were gaining footholds in Europe, the world-wide Great Depression of the late 1920s and early 1930s was slowly paving a road to militarization in both Europe and Japan.

At the same time, the raise of chauvinistic ideology and fascism was foreshadowing the outbreak of World War II, first in Europe and then in Japan.

Azurian solutions are tailored to the needs of each client business, designed to enhance performance and profitability, achieve competitive advantage and sustain market leadership.

Approach

Azurian projects are unique to each client but they share a common element – visible value creation. In addition to an expertly designed web presence that raises visibility in the marketplace and serves as a window into a business, our team develops business strategies and e-business applications that are focused on creating operational efficiencies and revenue streams.

We approach the challenges facing each business with an eIDEA. Azurian's eIDEA is a systematic, but flexible methodology that guides the development of our solutions to complex business problems. The process facilitates communication at crucial junctures, minimizes cost, time and risk for our clients and ensures quality and consistency in our deliverables.

ing a formal description of the discontinuities that can occur in the determined phenomena, causing them to take unexpected forms." The theory thus provides the tools to understand phenomena previously unexplainable through linear models.

Otherness in Aesthetics

The following section discusses the problematics of "otherness" in aesthetic discourse. It shall confront the issue of artistic production on two levels: content — in connection with the rise of new aesthetic categories — and the adequate representation of that content through form.

The "Other" and the Emergence of New Aesthetic Categories

As previously discussed, Craig Owen's theory of allegory is the most visible manifestation of a tendency toward the "other" in the arts. Architectural theories such as Kenneth Frampton's *critical regionalism* also reveal an interest in local difference outside universal modernism.

"...Critical Regionalism is a dialectical expression. It self-consciously seeks to deconstruct universal modernism in terms of values and images which are locally cultivated, while at the same time adulterating these autochthonous elements with paradigms drawn from alien sources...Critical Regionalism recognizes that no living tradition remains available to modern man other than the subtle procedures of synthetic contradiction."(K. Frampton, "Prospects for a Critical Regionalism," *Perspecta* 20:149).

In an epistemic sense, the "other" may be understood as the different, the nonrepresentable, the distant in space and time, and the fragment. In this connection, the link between "otherness" and theories of *allegory, regionalism*, and the notion of the *sublime*—that which is incommensurable and unrepresentatble — becomes possible.

The Sublime as the Representation of the "Other"

The centrality of the idea of the sublime in recent aesthetic discourse can be linked to the distinctly postmodern concern for difference and for the "incommensurable." In contemporary criticism, primarily in the theories of Lyotard[8] and Jameson,[9] there has been a reassessment of the idea of the *sublime* based on the 18th century formulations of Burke and Kant.

The relevance of the idea of the sublime in artistic practice lies in the tension between the desire for representation and the difficulty of that representation due, for instance, to immensity of scale, quantity of data, or inavailabilty of information. Such tension could create a "force field" for artistic production reflecting a fascination for the distant and the incommensurable both in space and time.

Column one
Detail of an exhibit panel with text set on three, two, and one of nine columns.

Page layout with text set on five, three, and one of eight columns.

Column two
Page layout with text set on four, three, and two of twelve columns.

2

Transformation of information

The basic principles of typographic design transform the utilitarian quality of words, lines, paragraphs and columns into an aesthetic form that conveys both the intellectual meaning and emotional feeling of the message. Typography supports reading, but it is also a source of aesthetic pleasure and inspiration.

Through the relationship between the elements and space, the proportion of elements to one another, and their rhythm and composition, design not only objectively conveys information but also gives subjective cues for the interpretation of its contents.

To transform even the simplest piece of information into a sophisticated message, the typographic designer relies on theories and aesthetic principles developed over centuries. To produce vital work, these design principles will always be essential.

Space

Space is an essential, but ambivalent, component of typography. On the one hand, space provides the necessary background for the typographic elements that will occupy it; on the other hand, space is precious and needs to be preserved.

This ambivalence makes space inhibiting as well. At first, space without elements appears large. Later, after the first few elements are placed, the space seems too small for still more elements to come.

Space is simultaneously many things: the format, the background, the separation of elements, and the counter forms. Space is the common ground in design, from the simplest to the most complex composition.

In typographic design space is two-dimensional, defined by two horizontals and two verticals. The two dimensions determine the size and proportion of space.

A typographic element derives its optical qualities from its relationship to the boundaries of the space it is placed in. The position, direction or intervals of typographic elements are perceived in relation to the boundaries of the space. Depending on its position in relation to the boundaries, the element appears to be moving left,

The form of space contributes to how typography is perceived; it supports the content of typography.

Square, horizontal and vertical rectangles of identical size. Proportion and orientation determine the difference in their appearance.

Triangular, circular and rhombic space. Each space has a strong expression that is incompatible with orthogonal typography.

Arrow-shaped space, a hybrid of a rectangle and an equilateral triangle.

right, up, or down; or it may appear to be optically advancing or receding.

The dimension and form of space both limits and expands the expressiveness of typography. It limits the number and position of elements because the space is defined and finite; it expands because the form of space complements the arrangement of the typographic elements or text.

The form of space has an expression; it influences how we perceive typography. The horizontal format has a different expression than the vertical format.

In typographic design the predominant shape of space is square or rectangular. Because of its strong horizontal and vertical orientation, typography is difficult to position in a triangular, circular, or rhombic space. The arrow-shaped space based on a rectangle and an equilateral triangle, is an example of a hybrid space.

Column one
US standard letterhead, 8.5x11 in.

US No.10 standard envelope, 9.5x4.125 in.

US standard postcard, 6x4.25 in.

US standard business card, 3.5x2 in.

Column two
8.5x11 in. letterhead folded into thirds, 8.5x3.67 in.

11x8.5 in. folded in half, 5.5x8.5 in.

Credit card 3.375x2.125 in.

Standard space

The character of space derives from its size and from the proportion, or relationship, of its two dimensions. Typographic design begins by deciding the size and proportion of the space, which may be a standard format or a constructed space.

The standard space applies to letterhead, envelopes, business- and postcards, forms, brochures and business documents that must be economically produced and efficiently stored.

Constructed space applies to posters, catalogs, and books, items produced outside the mainstream of business.

Constructed space is based on rational proportions such as 1:2, 2:3, 3:4, or classical proportions such as 1:1.414 (the DIN standard sizes) or 1:1.618 (the Golden Section).

The standard size for letterhead, business documents and brochures is 8.5x11 in. in the USA and 210x297 mm (DIN A4) in Europe and Asia.

The standard size for envelopes is 9.5x4.125 in. (No.10) in the USA and 224x114 mm (DIN C6/5) in Europe and Asia.

The standard size for postcards is 4.25x6 in. in the USA and 105x148 mm (DIN A6) in Europe and Asia.

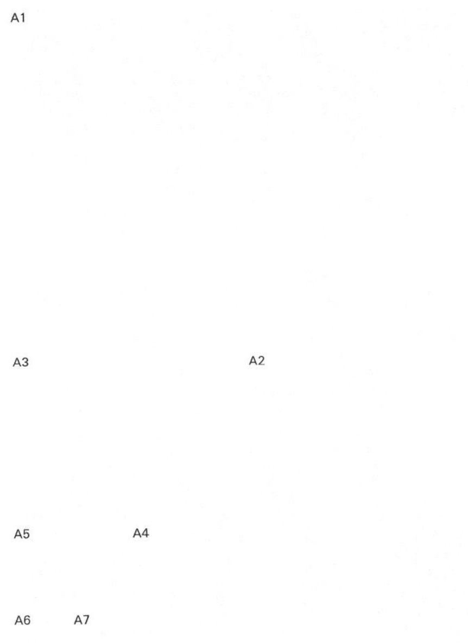

A1

A3 A2

A5 A4

A6 A7

Column one
DIN A4 letterhead, 210x297 mm, used in Europe and Asia.

DIN C6/5 envelope, 224x114 mm.

DIN A6 postcard, 148x105 mm.

While the US business card size of 3.5x2 in. (89x51 mm) is also used in Europe and Asia, there are no standard sizes.

4x5 in. transparency, proportion 4:5.

35 mm slide, proportion 3:2.

Column two
The DIN standard size construction. Each format has the proportion of 1:1.414.
A0 = 841x1189 mm
A1 = 594x841
A2 = 420x594
A3 = 297x420
A4 = 210x297
A5 = 148x210
A6 = 105x148
A7 = 74x105

Monitor screen, proportion 4:3.

The standard size for business cards in the USA is 3.5x2 in. While this size is also common outside the USA, there are no standard business card sizes in other countries.

Folding transforms standard space into smaller standard sizes. Common smaller sizes derive from folding the standard 11x8.5 in. size in half to 5.5x8.5 in., or into thirds to 3.67x8.5 in.

The fact that letterheads always fold into thirds and appear as an interrupted space is an important consideration in stationery design.

Other standard spaces in design are the 4x5 in. transparency (proportion 4:5); the 35 mm slide, (proportion 3:2); and the monitor screen (proportion 4:3).

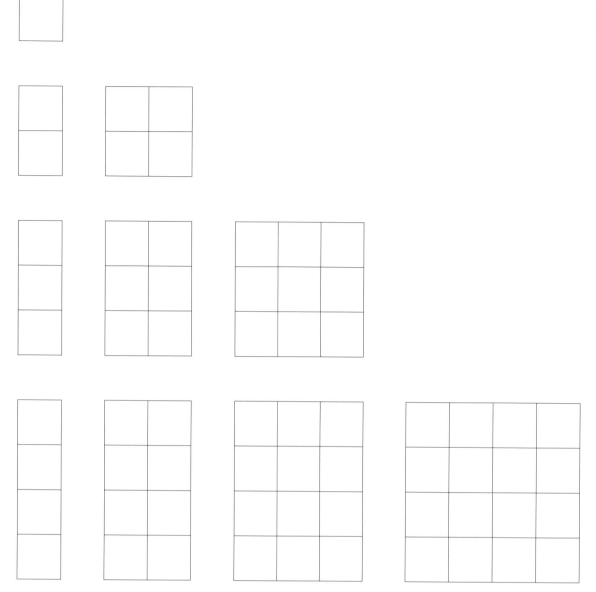

Common rational proportions based on a square unit.

Constructed space

Constructed space is characterized by a series of integral subdivisions. Instead of confronting a blank space, the designer proceeds from the implied subdivisions.

The basis for constructed space is the square. Square units combine to form space with rational proportions, such as 1:2, 2:3, and 3:4. A large number of different proportions can be created this way.

A classical, widely used proportion for constructed space is the Golden Section, which divides space in proportions of 1:1.618. The construction is based on a square horizontally divided in half. The diagonal of the upper half of the square is rotated to determine the vertical side of the rectangle.

Another classical proportion for constructed space is 1:1.414. The construction is based on a square whose diagonal is rotated to determine the vertical side of the rectangle.

Le Corbusier expanded the Golden Section with his Modulor proportion system. In the Modulor, the basic unit is a human figure 183 cm (six foot) tall divided in the proportion of 1:1.618 (70:113 cm). These proportions determined the sizes of the Red Series: 27, 43, 70, 113, 183, 296 and so on. A second basic unit of 226 cm

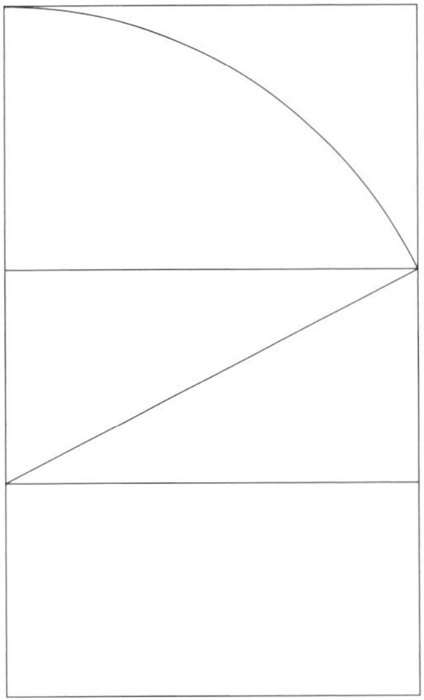

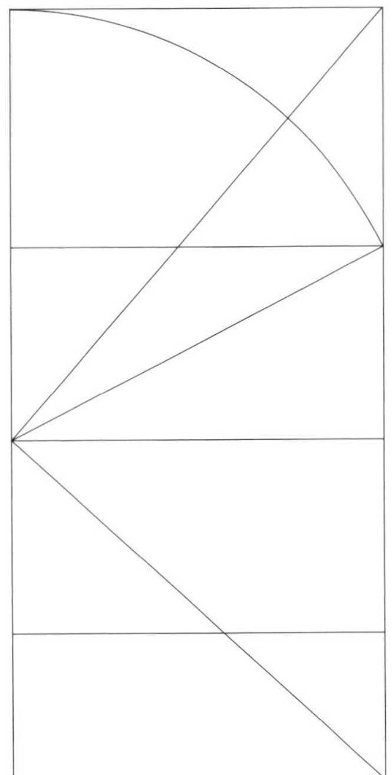

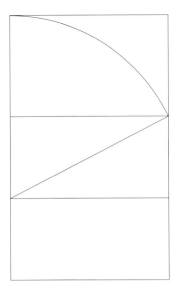

Constructed space, proportion 1:1.618, Golden Section.

Constructed space, proportion 1:1.414.

Modulor construction.

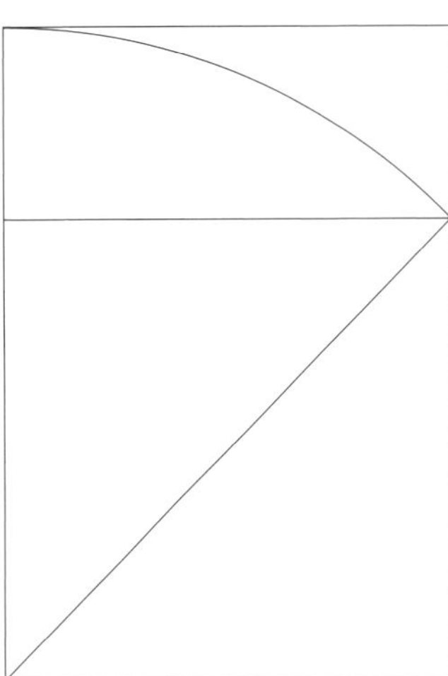

(two 113 cm squares, or the human figure with raised arm) produces the Blue Series: 20, 33, 53, 86,140, 226, and so on.

Because of its inherent horizontal and vertical subdivisions, a space with the rational proportions of 1:2, 2:3 or 3:4 is more useful to the designer than a constructed space with the classical proportions. Classical spaces contain only one or two horizontal subdivisions that can be utilized in the design.

Elementary subdivisions transform space. By folding, two-dimensional space transforms into space that implies a third dimension.

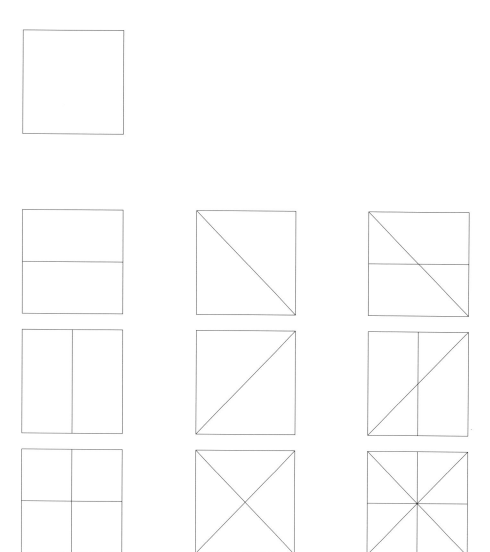

Transformed space

Inherent in every space is a series of elementary and logical subdivisions. Folded in half horizontally or vertically, the square is transformed into two rectangles proportioned 1:2; folding diagonally yields two triangles proportioned 1:1.414. Folded in such a way, the square surface is transformed into an implied three-dimensional form.

The square-based rectangular space folded diagonally implies a third dimension; parts of the back of the space are revealed. The concept of geometrically transforming space contributed to the design of the posters on pages 135, 144, 146, 148, 150, 152.

Examples of a square and two square-based rectangles folded, implying three-dimensional space.

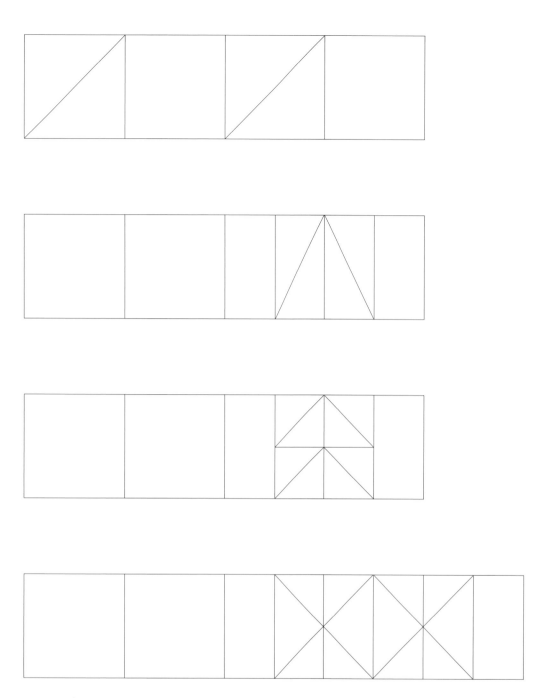

Diagrams for four announcements and season's greetings cards.

The cards are based on 4.5 x 4.5 in. modules folded at 45 and 60 degrees.

A series of announcements and season's greetings cards based on 4.5 x 4.5 in. modules of folded and plain space. The effect of the combined two- and three-dimensional space is stronger than the typographic message it carries.

In essence, each card transforms from a two-dimensional into a three-dimensional space. Typography is secondary in conveying the message.

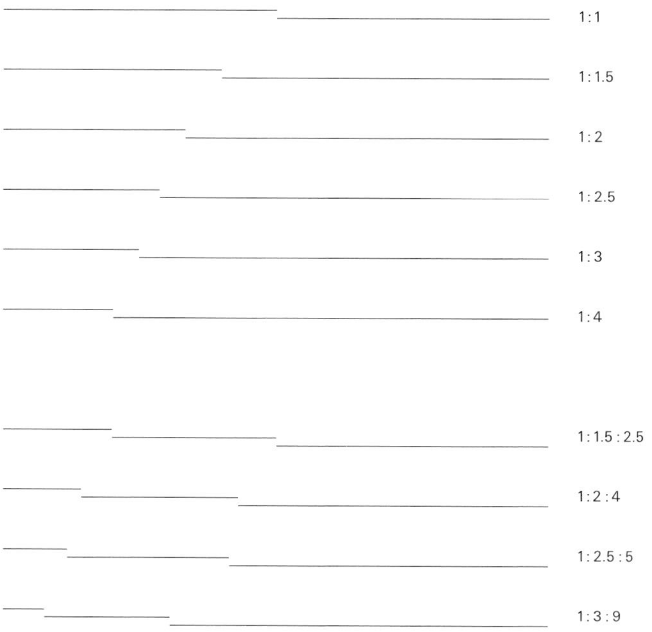

1:1

1:1.5

1:2

1:2.5

1:3

1:4

1:1.5 : 2.5

1:2 : 4

1:2.5 : 5

1:3 : 9

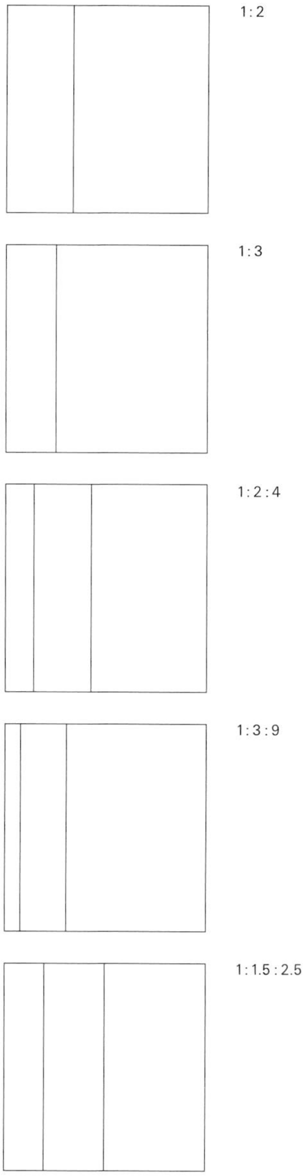

1:2

1:3

1:2 : 4

1:3 : 9

1:1.5 : 2.5

Rules divided into two and three parts of different proportions.

Square space divided into two and three parts of different proportions.

Proportion

Proportion defines the relation of individual parts to one another and to the whole. In typographic design, proportions are fundamental; ambiguous or weak proportions, lacking tension and contrast, lead to monotonous, uninspiring results.

Fundamental proportions include the size and proportion of the space and the scale and proportion of the typographic elements positioned in that space.

Proportions shape design at both the macro- and microaesthetic level. At the macroaesthetic level, important proportions include space width to height, the horizontal and vertical subdivisions of the space, the negative space to information, the proportion of colors, and the proportion of type sizes. At the microaesthetic level, the proportion of letterform height to width, form to counter form, capital height to x-height, type size to line space, and paragraph indent to column width influence the optical quality of typography.

Proportions are experienced on both an intellectual and emotional level. On an intellectual level, proportions are perceived as final, measurable, rational, calculated, and constructed. They invite analysis. On an emotional

Column one
Letterform proportions at the microaesthetic level.

Height to width.

Form to counterform.

Crossbar position to vertical dimension.

i-dot to stem.

Column two
The proportions of cap-height, x-height, ascenders, and descenders contribute to the character of each typeface.

level, proportions appear open-ended, fluid, rhythmic, alive, changeable, and open to interpretation. They provide aesthetic pleasure.

Proportions, as with all aesthetics, are subjective to some extent. The ideal proportions can neither be rationalized nor proven, nor are they universal. Every designer has a slightly different, personal sense of proportion; experienced designers develop the proportions appropriate for the intended design on a case-by-case basis.

Proportions are established by empirical criteria or developed on a mathematical basis. Establishing proportions based on empirical criteria, that is by relying on experience or observation without regard for a system or theory, requires sensitivity, intuition, and judgment.

The concise, calibrated range of type sizes, defined in pica, points or in millimeters, is conducive to establishing mathematical proportions. The proportional relation of type size and interline space is established through their numeric value. For instance, the proportion of 8 point type to 10 point interline space (1:1.25) is decisive and clear, and optically more pleasing than the arbitrary proportion of 8 point type to 10.35 point interline space.

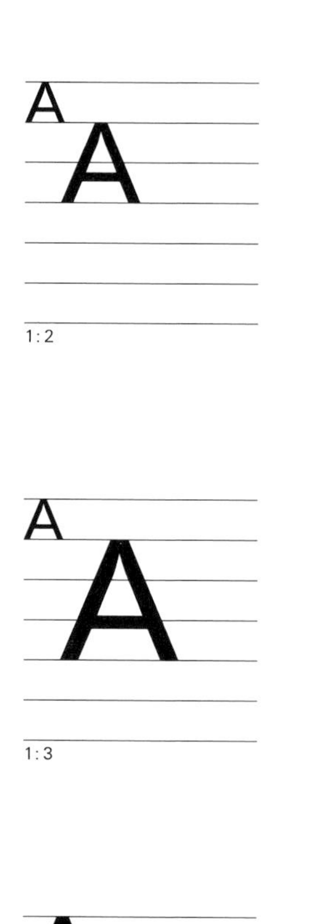

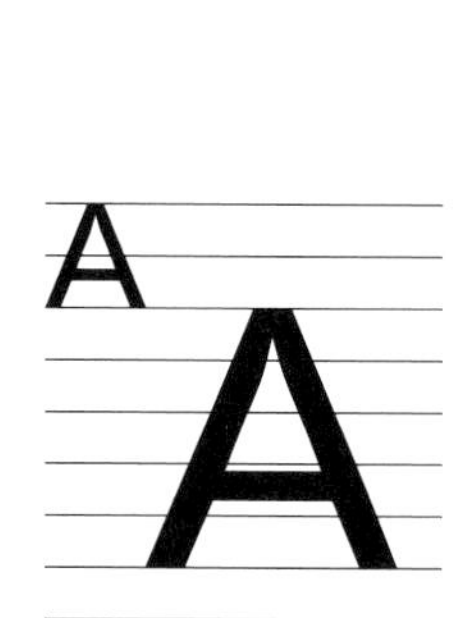

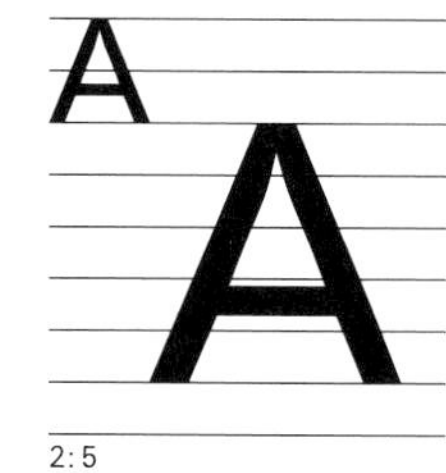

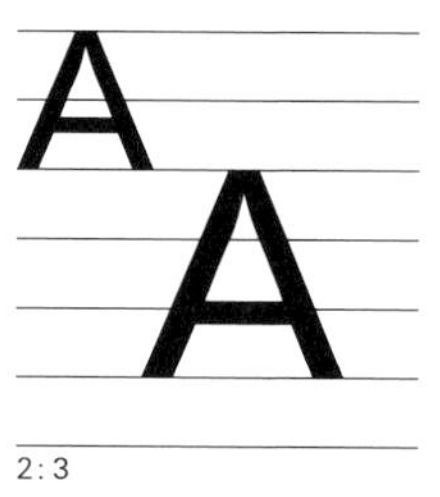

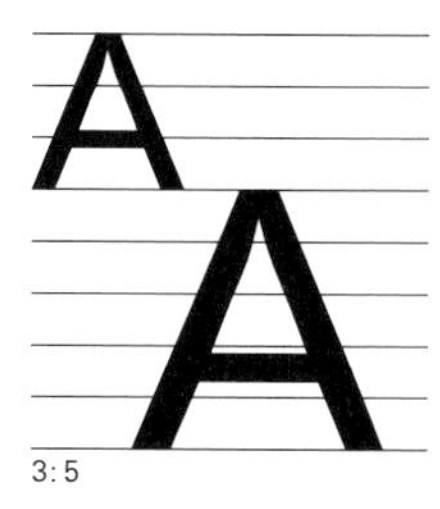

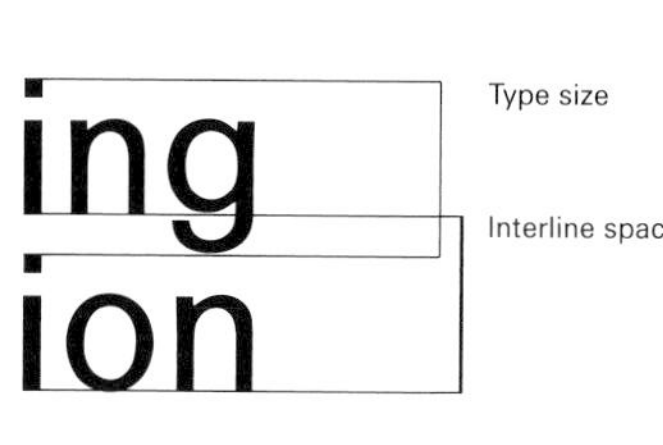

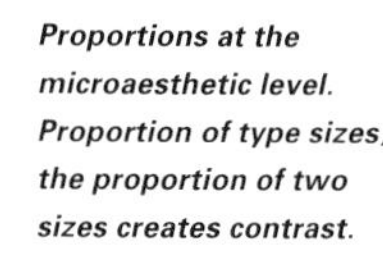

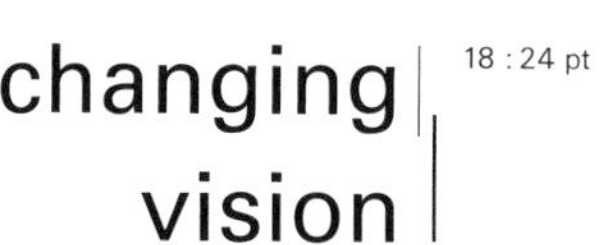

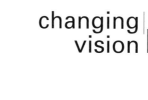

Proportions at the microaesthetic level. Proportion of type sizes; the proportion of two sizes creates contrast.

Innumerable proportions derive from the calibrated range of type sizes from 6 to 72 point.

The proportion of type size to interline space dramatically changes the optical value of type *(see also page 56)*.

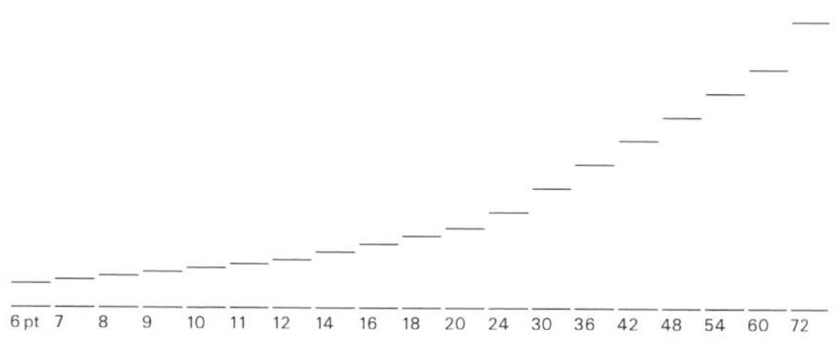

For the typographic designer, the keys to developing mathematical proportions are adhering to the numerical values of the typographic material, an appreciation and understanding of how these values relate, and an inclination for mathematics.

Although reliable to some extent, mathematical proportions cannot replace educated personal judgment or guarantee good design. They are merely a method, and because they can be easily summarized and communicated, I find them more reliable and efficient for large projects than empirically determined proportions.

The study of masterpieces of art and architecture reveals a close relation between mathematical and empirical proportions. However, it is futile to rationalize the proportions and apply calculated proportions to works created by great masters with unique talent, intuition, and passion.

Twenty-three miles from Agra in India, with its fabled Taj Mahal, lies Fatepur Sikri, a dream city built in sandstone the colors of the dying sunset. One approaches Fatepur Sikri in silence, for it has been deserted for over two hundred years, but immediately on entering the core of the city, the Mahal-i-Khas, the heart is uplifted, the eye entranced. One experiences a rare sensation of freedom and repose, an invitation to step forward buoyantly and, at the same time, to loiter luxuriously.

Wherever the eye turns the view is held, but at every step it changes. A seemingly solid background wall of stone is later perceived as a transparent screen. But nowhere is there a fixed center: nowhere a point from which the observer can dominate the whole. Equally nowhere does he stand conspicuously removed from the center, a spectator in the wings. From the moment he steps within this urban core he becomes an intimate part of the scene, which does not impose itself upon him, but discloses itself gradually to him, at his own pace and according to his own pleasure. The Mahal-i-Khas was the core of a city of perhaps fifty thousand people. It is a place somewhat larger than the Piazza San Marco in Venice and, like it, is framed by buildings and openings, as well as having buildings standing within it as objects, both dimensioning its own space and being set off by it. Despite un-

1 7

Twenty-three miles from Agra in India, with its fabled Taj Mahal, lies Fatepur Sikri, a dream city built in sandstone the colors of the dying sunset. One approaches Fatepur Sikri in silence, for it has been deserted for over two hundred years, but immediately on entering the core of the city, the Mahal-i-Khas, the heart is uplifted, the eye entranced. One experiences a rare sensation of freedom and repose, an invitation to step forward buoyantly and, at the same time, to loiter luxuriously. Wherever the eye turns the view is held, but at every step it changes. A seemingly

1 4

Twenty-three miles from Agra in India, with its fabled Taj Mahal, lies Fatepur Sikri, a dream city built in sandstone the colors of the dying sunset. One approaches Fatepur Sikri in silence, for it has been deserted for over two hundred years, but immediately on entering the core of the city, the Mahal-i-Khas, the heart is uplifted, the eye entranced. One experiences a rare sensation of freedom and repose, an invitation to step forward buoyantly and, at the same time, to loiter luxuriously. Wherever the eye turns the view is held, but at every step it changes. A seemingly solid background wall of stone is later perceived as a transparent screen. But nowhere is there a fixed center: nowhere a point from which the observer can dominate the whole. Equally nowhere does he stand conspicuously removed from the center, a spectator in the wings. From the

3 2

Twenty-three miles from Agra in India, with its fabled Taj Mahal, lies Fatepur Sikri, a dream city built in sandstone the colors of the dying sunset. One approaches Fatepur Sikri in silence, for it has been deserted for over two hundred years, but immediately on entering the core of the city, the Mahal-i-Khas, the heart is uplifted, the eye entranced. One experiences a rare sensation of freedom and repose, an invitation to step forward buoyantly and, at the same time, to loiter luxuriously.

Wherever the eye turns the view is held, but at every step it changes. A seemingly solid background wall of stone is later perceived as a transparent screen. But nowhere is there a fixed center: nowhere a point from which the observer can dominate the whole. Equally nowhere does he stand conspicuously removed from the center, a spectator in the wings. From the moment he steps within this urban core he becomes an intimate part of the scene, which does not impose itself upon him, but discloses itself gradually to him, at his own pace and according to his own pleasure. The Mahal-i-Khas was the core of a city of perhaps fifty thousand people. It is a place somewhat larger than the Piazza San Marco in Venice and, like it, is framed by buildings and openings, as well as having buildings standing within it as objects, both dimensioning its own space and being set off by it. Despite un-

1 5

Twenty-three miles from Agra in India, with its fabled Taj Mahal, lies Fatepur Sikri, a dream city built in sandstone the colors of the dying sunset. One approaches Fatepur Sikri in silence, for it has been deserted for over two hundred years, but immediately on entering the core of the city, the Mahal-i-Khas, the heart is uplifted, the eye entranced. One experiences a rare sensation of freedom and repose, an invitation to step forward buoyantly and, at the same time, to loiter luxuriously. Wherever the eye turns the view is held, but at every step it changes. A seemingly solid background wall of stone is later perceived as a transparent screen. But nowhere is there a fixed center: nowhere a point from which the observer can dominate the whole. Equally nowhere does he stand conspicuously removed from the center, a spectator in the wings. From the moment he steps within this urban core he becomes an intimate part of the scene, which does not impose itself upon him, but discloses itself gradually to him, at his own pace and according to his own pleasure. The Mahal-i-Khas was the core of a city of perhaps fifty thousand people. It is a

1 1

Twenty-three miles from Agra in India, with its fabled Taj Mahal, lies Fatepur Sikri, a dream city built in sandstone the colors of the dying sunset. One approaches Fatepur Sikri in silence, for it has been deserted for over two hundred years, but immediately on entering the core of the city, the Mahal-i-Khas, the heart is uplifted, the eye entranced. One experiences a rare sensation of freedom and repose, an invitation to step forward buoyantly and, at the same time, to loiter luxuriously. Wherever the eye turns the view is held, but at every step it changes. A seemingly solid background wall of stone is later perceived as a transparent screen. But nowhere is there a fixed center: nowhere a point from which the observer can dominate the whole. Equally nowhere does he stand conspicuously removed from the center, a spectator in the wings. From the moment he steps within this urban core he becomes an intimate part of the scene, which does not impose itself upon him, but discloses itself gradually to him, at his own pace and according to his own pleasure. The Mahal-i-Khas was the core of a city of perhaps fifty thousand people. It is a place somewhat larger than the Piazza San Marco in Venice and, like it, is framed by buildings and openings, as well as having buildings standing within it as objects, both dimensioning its own space and being set off by it.

3 5

Twenty-three miles from Agra in India, with its fabled Taj Mahal, lies Fatepur Sikri, a dream city built in sandstone the colors of the dying sunset. One approaches Fatepur Sikri in silence, for it has been deserted for over two hundred years, but immediately on entering the core of the city, the Mahal-i-Khas, the heart is uplifted, the eye entranced. One experiences a rare sensation of freedom and repose, an invitation to step forward buoyantly and, at the same time, to loiter luxuriously.

Wherever the eye turns the view is held, but at every step it changes. A seemingly solid background wall of stone is later perceived as a transparent screen. But nowhere is there a fixed center: nowhere a point from which the observer can dominate the whole. Equally nowhere does he stand conspicuously removed from the center, a spectator in the wings. From the moment he steps within this urban core he becomes an intimate part of the scene, which does not impose itself upon him, but discloses itself gradually to him, at his own pace and according to his own pleasure. The Mahal-i-Khas was the core of a city of perhaps fifty thousand people. It is a place somewhat larger than the Piazza San Marco in Venice and, like it, is framed by buildings and openings, as well as having buildings standing within it as objects, both dimensioning its own space and being set off by it. Despite un-

1 3

Twenty-three miles from Agra in India, with its fabled Taj Mahal, lies Fatepur Sikri, a dream city built in sandstone the colors of the dying sunset. One approaches Fatepur Sikri in silence, for it has been deserted for over two hundred years, but immediately on entering the core of the city, the Mahal-i-Khas, the heart is uplifted, the eye entranced. One experiences a rare sensation of freedom and repose, an invitation to step forward buoyantly and, at the same time, to loiter luxuriously. Wherever the eye turns the view is held, but at every step it changes. A seemingly solid background wall of stone is later perceived as a transparent screen. But nowhere is there a fixed center: nowhere a point from which the observer can dominate the whole. Equally nowhere does he stand conspicuously removed from the center, a spectator in the wings. From the moment he steps within this urban core he becomes an intimate part of the scene, which does not impose itself upon him, but discloses itself gradually to him, at his own pace and according to his own pleasure. The Mahal-i-Khas was the core of a city of perhaps fifty thousand people. It is a place somewhat larger than the Piazza San Marco in Venice and, like it, is framed by buildings and openings, as well as having buildings standing within it as objects, both dimensioning its own space and being set off by it. Despite un-Western details of architectural ornament, the contemporary visitor to Fatepur Sikri is at once struck by the likeness of the spatial composition of these solids and voids in the Mahal-i-Khas to our modern Western thinking about the interplay of freedom and enclosure, transparency and repose. Nothing in this deserted city of Fatepur Sikri is fortuitous,

3 1

Twenty-three miles from Agra in India, with its fabled Taj Mahal, lies Fatepur Sikri, a dream city built in sandstone the colors of the dying sunset. One approaches Fatepur Sikri in silence, for it has been deserted for over two hundred years, but immediately on entering the core of the city, the Mahal-i-Khas, the heart is uplifted, the eye entranced. One experiences a rare sensation of freedom and repose, an invitation to step forward buoyantly and, at the same time, to loiter luxuriously. Wherever the eye turns the view is held, but at every step it changes. A seemingly solid background wall of stone is later perceived as a transparent screen. But nowhere is there a fixed center: nowhere a point from which the observer can dominate the whole. Equally nowhere does he stand conspicuously removed from the center, a spectator in the wings. From the moment he steps within this urban core he becomes an intimate part of the scene, which does not impose itself upon him, but discloses itself gradually to him, at his own pace and according to his own pleasure. The Mahal-i-Khas was the core of a city of perhaps fifty thousand people. It is a place somewhat larger than the Piazza San Marco in Venice and, like it, is framed by buildings and openings, as well as having buildings standing within it as objects, both dimensioning its own space and being set off by it. Despite un-Western details of architectural ornament, the contemporary visitor to Fatepur Sikri is at once struck by the likeness of the spatial composition of these solids and voids in the Mahal-i-Khas to our modern Western thinking about the interplay of freedom and enclosure, transparency and repose. Nothingin this deserted city of Fatepur Sikri is fortuitous, and none of the effects are due either to the accretions of time or to its ravages. The city was built at one stroke by Akbar the

1 5

Proportions at the micro-aesthetic level. Proportion of paragraph indent to column width. The clearly defined paragraph indent is part of the typographic structure and provides an alignment for folios and subtitles.

Proportions at the macro-aesthetic level. Proportion of printed to white space. The optical quality of typography depends on the decisive proportion of occupied to empty space.

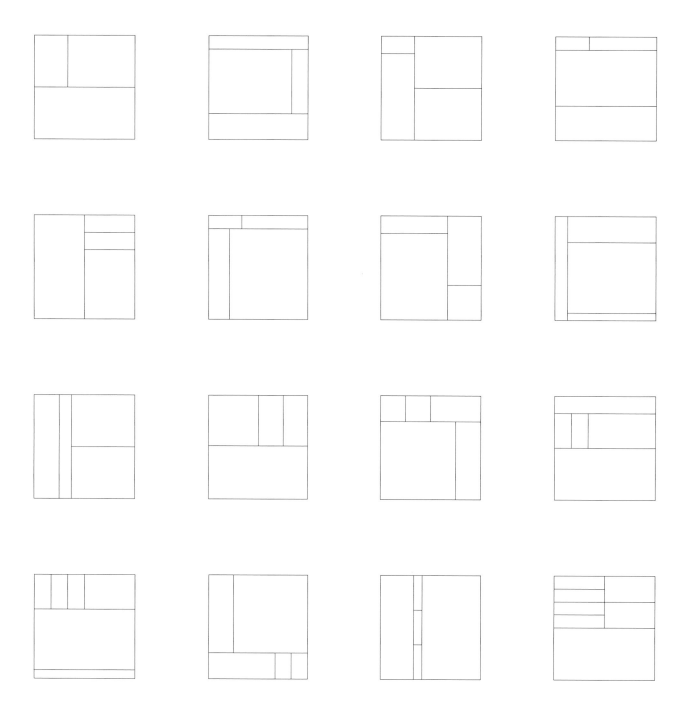

A square space is subdivided in different proportions. The variations derive from a series of intuitive development sketches that were refined into rational proportions. There is a close correlation between the intuitive and the rational proportions.

Twenty-three miles from Agra in India, with its fabled Taj Mahal, lies Fatepur Sikri, a dream city built in sandstone the colors of the dying sunset. One approaches Fatepur Sikri in silence, for it has been deserted for over two hundred years, but immediately on entering the core of the city, the Mahal-i-Khas, the heart is uplifted, the eye entranced. One experiences a rare sensation of freedom and repose, an invitation to step forward buoyantly and, at the same time, to loiter luxuriously. Wherever the eye turns the view is held, but at every step it changes. A seemingly solid background wall of stone is later perceived as a transparent screen. But nowhere is there a fixed center: nowhere a point from which the observer can dominate the whole. Equally nowhere does he stand conspicuously removed from the center, a spectator in the wings. From the moment he steps within this urban core he becomes an intimate part of the scene, which does not impose itself upon him, but discloses itself gradually to him, at his own pace and according to his own

1 / 7.5 / 1.5

3 | 6 | 1

3 / 1

The primary aim of the core studios is to develop the capacity of the student to conceptualize thought into architectural form at all levels of making, from the detail to the building, and from the building to the city.

2 | 1

Twenty-three miles from Agra in India, with its fabled Taj Mahal, lies Fatepur Sikri, a dream city built in sandstone the colors of the dying sunset. One approaches Fatepur Sikri in silence, for it has been deserted for over two hundred years, but immediately on entering the core of the city, the Mahal-i-Khas, the heart is uplifted, the eye entranced. One experiences a rare sensation of freedom and repose, an invitation to step forward buoyantly and, at the same time, to loiter luxuriously. Wherever the eye turns the view is held, but at every step it changes. A seemingly solid background wall of stone is later perceived as a transparent screen. But nowhere is there a fixed center: nowhere a point from which the observer can dominate the whole. Equally nowhere does he stand conspicuously removed from the center, a spectator in the wings. From the moment he steps within this urban core he becomes an intimate part of the scene, which

1 / 7.5 / 1.5

1 | 5 | 3

1 / 6 / 6

3 | 9 | 1

The primary aim of the core studios is to develop the capacity of the student to conceptualize thought into architectural form at all levels of making, from the detail to the building, and from the building to the city.

1 | 5 | 6

Twenty-three miles from Agra in India, with its fabled Taj Mahal, lies Fatepur Sikri, a dream city built in sandstone the colors of the dying sunset. One approaches Fatepur Sikri in silence, for it has been deserted for over two hundred years, but immediately on entering the core of the city, the Mahal-i-Khas, the heart is uplifted, the eye entranced. One experiences a rare sensation of freedom and repose, an invitation to step forward buoyantly and, at the same time, to loiter luxuriously. Wherever the eye turns the view is held, but at every step it changes. A seemingly solid background wall of stone is later perceived as a transparent screen. But nowhere is there a fixed center: nowhere a point from which the observer can dominate the whole. Equally nowhere does he stand conspicuously removed from the center, a spectator in the wings. From the moment he steps within this urban core he becomes an intimate part of the scene, which does not impose itself upon

1 / 7 / 5

1 | 10 | 2

1 / 9 / 3

3 | 6 | 1

2 / 1

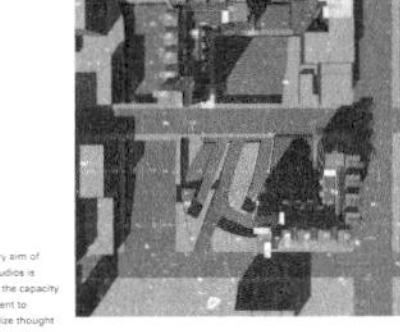

The primary aim of the core studios is to develop the capacity of the student to conceptualize thought into architectural form at all levels of making, from the detail to the building, and from the building to the city.

1 | 2 | 7

Proportions at the macro-aesthetic level. Margin proportions determine the position of text or photographs on the page. Carefully developed margin proportions enhance the information.

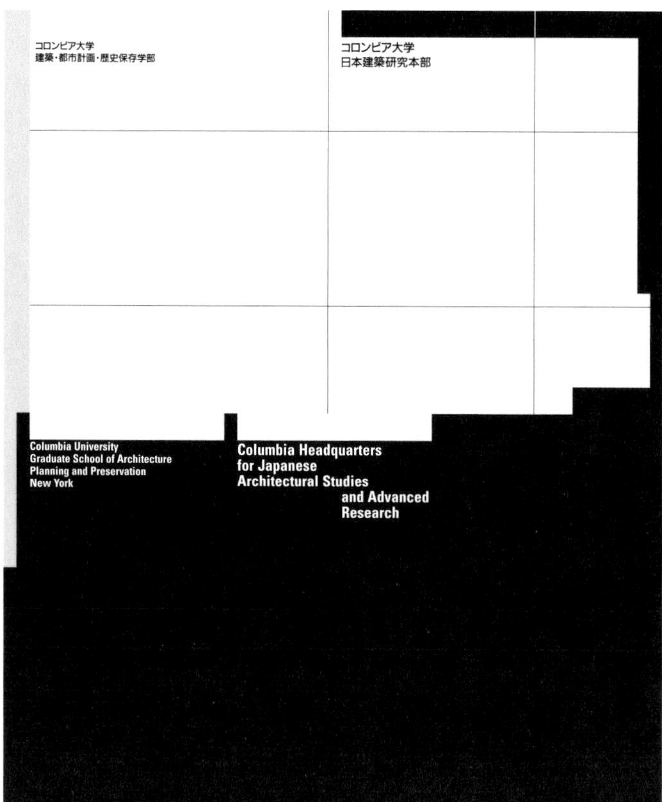

Evening Lectures
Andrew MacNair
Mark Rakatansky
Harry Kendall
Reinhold Martin
Karl Chu

Symposium
The Multi-Scaled Site: Learning from Lower Manhattan

Lunchtime Lectures
Peter Marcuse
Robert Beauregard
Esra Akcan
Jeffrey Raven
Nader Vossoughian
Hernan Diaz-Alonso
George Thrush
Charles Lyle
Claire Weisz

Columbia
Architecture
Planning
Preservation

Films

Brochure cover.
This design is based on the decisive proportion of black to white space.
The subdivisions of the white space derive from the brochure's internal structure.

Poster for a summer program in architecture.
The different proportions of black distinguish the four parts of the program.

Bernard Tschumi, Dean
Graduate School of Architecture
Planning, and Preservation

on the occasion of the
NAAB Accreditation Team's visit to the
Master of Architecture Program

invites you to an exhibition of

Reception and viewing
Monday, March 26
6:00–7:30pm

Arthur Ross Architecture Gallery
Buell Hall
Columbia University

Student 1998
Work: -2000

Columbia University
in the City of New York
Graduate School of Architecture Planning and Preservation
Commencement Ceremony
2:00pm
Wednesday, May 22
St. Paul's Chapel
Admit one

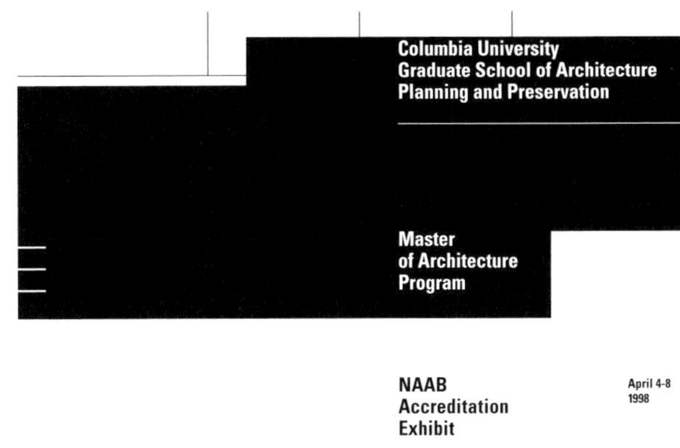

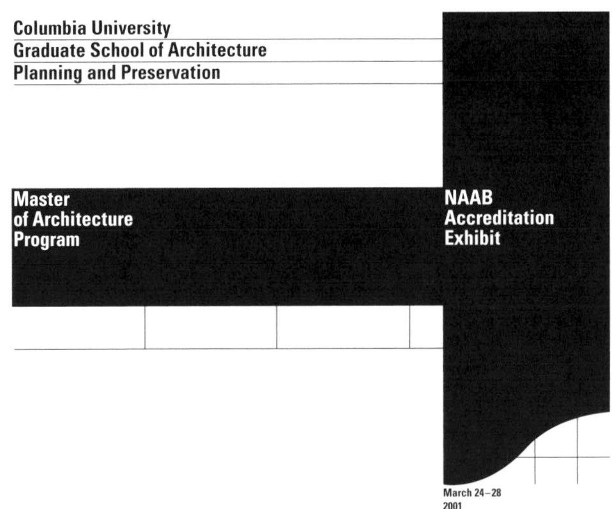

Invitation to an exhibition of student work. This design is based on the 1:3 proportion of the gray band to background.

Admission ticket. The square's horizontal and vertical dimension are subdivided in the proportion of 1:1.5.

Cover for an architectural publication. This design is based on the proportion of black band to background. All subdivisions of the space derive from the publication's internal structure.

Cover for an architectural publication. Rotated at 90 degrees, the black T-shape divides the background in strong contrasting proportions. All subdivisions of the space derive from the publication's internal structure.

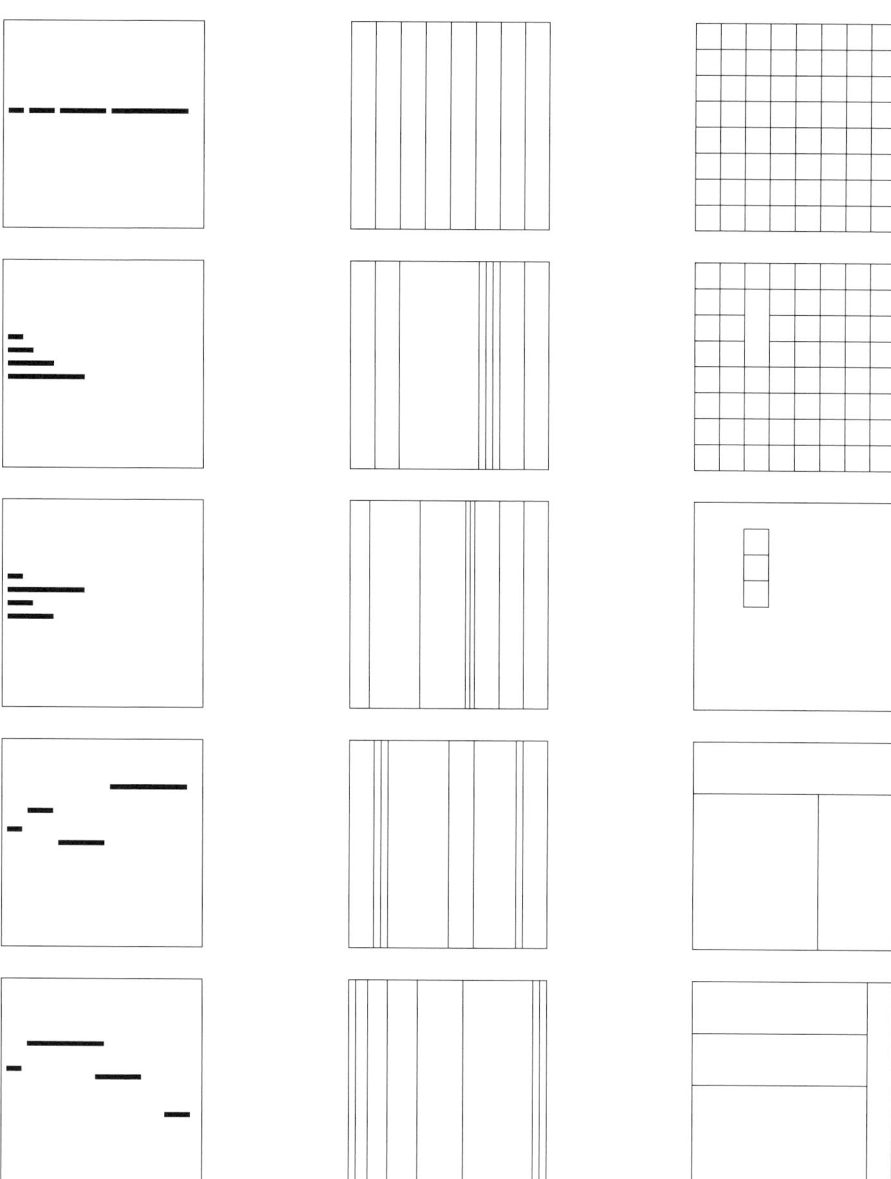

Column one
Four different length lines create a subtle horizontal rhythm.

Animated rhythms created by different arrangements of lines.

Column two
Equally spaced vertical lines create a monotonous rhythm.

Animated rhythms created by shifting and clustering the lines.

Column three
Square grid with monotonous rhythm.

White space emphasizes the rhythm.

Rhythm created by subdividing the space.

Rhythm

Rhythm is inherent in every detail of typography. The configuration of strokes creates the rhythm of a letter; letterform and space determine the rhythm of a word; words and word spaces form the rhythm of a line; and lines and interline space create the rhythm of a text.

In typography, rhythm is not experienced as an isolated visual sensation. It is part of a larger composition of elements and affects the entire space. Two typographic elements placed in a space create a subtle rhythm; further subdividing a space results in smaller units that create a rhythm within that space.

Rhythm is created by the repetition or alternation of visual elements. Rhythm can be predictable, like a pattern, or animated and progressive, created through the movement and counter-movement of elements. The rhythm's strength affects the expression of the whole design.

Rhythm is essential for attracting and keeping the viewer's attention. The rhythm created through a simple repetition of elements soon becomes monotonous and tiring.

A line pattern with regular intervals, or a square grid, is optically static. A static pattern attracts, but does not maintain, attention. An effective rhythm depends on the

India

Twenty-three miles from Agra in India

I n d i a

Twenty-three miles from Agra in India

I n d i a

Twenty-three miles from Agra in India

I n d i a

Twenty-three miles from Agra in India

In di a

Twenty-three miles from Agra in India

Column one
Word rhythm.
Letterforms and letter space create word rhythm.

Changing the letter space alters word rhythm.

Column two
Line rhythm.
The word length and word space create line rhythm.

The words' length determines the rhythm of word spaces.

Changing the word space alters line rhythm.

Word space may be used to emphasize individual words or word groups in a line.

variation of positions, weights, sizes, or number of typographic elements.

In typographic communication rhythm stimulates both the mind and the eye. An effective rhythm is progressive and changing; its strength is defined by the optical sensation it evokes. However, an effective rhythm depends on both action and relief. Excessive rhythm without relief fatigues the reader.

Twenty-three miles from Agra in India, with its fabled Taj Mahal lies Fatepur Sikri, a dream city built in sandstone the colors of the dying sunset. One approaches Fatepur Sikri in silence, for it has been deserted for over two hundred years, but immediately on entering the core of the city, the Mahal-i-Khas, the heart is up lifted, the eye entranced. One experiences a rare sensation of freedom and repose, an invitation to step forward buoyantly and at the same time, to loiter luxuriously. Wherever the eye turns the view is held, but at every step it changes. A seemingly solid background wall of stone is later perceived as a transparent scr een. But nowhere is there a fixed center: nowhere a point from which the observer can dominate the whole. Equally now here does he stand conspicuously removed from the center, a specta

Twenty-three miles from Agra in India, with its fabled Taj Mahal lies Fatepur Sikri, a dream city built in sandstone the colors of the dying sunset. One approaches Fatepur Sikri in silence, for it has been deserted for over two hundred years, but immediately on entering the core of the city, the Mahal-i-Khas, the heart is up lifted, the eye entranced. One experiences a rare sensation of freedom and repose, an invitation to step forward buoyantly and at the same time, to loiter luxuriously. Wherever the eye turns the view is held, but at every step it changes. A seemingly solid background wall of stone is later perceived as a transparent scr

Twenty-three miles from Agra in India, with its fabled Taj Mahal lies Fatepur Sikri, a dream city built in sandstone the colors of the dying sunset. One approaches Fatepur Sikri in silence, for it has been deserted for over two hundred years, but immediately on entering the core of the city, the Mahal-i-Khas, the heart is up lifted, the eye entranced. One experiences a rare sensation of freedom and repose, an invitation to step forward buoyantly and

Twenty-three miles from Agra in India, with its fabled Taj Mahal lies Fatepur Sikri, a dream city built in sandstone the colors of the dying sunset. One approaches Fatepur Sikri in silence, for it has been deserted for over two hundred years, but immediately on entering the core of the city, the Mahal-i-Khas, the heart is up

Twenty-three miles from Agra in India, with its fabled Taj Mahal lies Fatepur Sikri, a dream city built in sandstone the colors of the dying sunset. One approaches Fatepur Sikri in silence, for it has been deserted for over two hundred years, but immediately on entering the core of the city, the Mahal-i-Khas, the heart is up lifted, the eye entranced. One experiences a rare sensation of freedom and repose, an invitation to step forward buoyantly and at the same time, to loiter luxuriously. Wherever the eye turns the view is held, but at every step it changes. A seemingly solid background wall of stone is later perceived as a transparent scr een. But nowhere is there a fixed center: nowhere a point from which the observer can dominate the whole. Equally now here does he stand conspicuously removed from the center, a specta

Twenty-three miles from Agra in India, with its fabled
Taj Mahal, lies Fatepur Sikri, a dream city built in sandstone
the colors of the dying sunset. One approaches Fatepur
Sikri in silence, for it has been deserted for over two hundred
years, but immediately on entering the core of the city,
the Mahal-i-Khas, the heart is uplifted, the eye entranced.
One experiences a rare sensation of freedom and repose, an
invitation to step forward buoyantly and, at the same
time, to loiter luxuriously. Wherever the eye turns the view
is held, but at every step it changes. A seemingly solid
background wall of stone is later perceived as a transparent
screen. But nowhere is there a fixed center: nowhere
a point from which the observer can dominate the whole.

Twenty-three miles from Agra in India,
with its fabled Taj Mahal,
lies Fatepur Sikri,
a dream city built in sandstone the colors of the dying sunset.
One approaches Fatepur Sikri in silence,
for it has been deserted for over two hundred years,
but immediately on entering the core of the city,
the Mahal-i-Khas,
the heart is uplifted,
the eye entranced.
One experiences a rare sensation of freedom and repose,
an invitation to step forward buoyantly and,
at the same time,

Twenty-three
miles
from
Agra
in
India,
with
its
fabled
Taj
Mahal,
lies
Fatepur

Column one
Text rhythm.
Text with uniform interline space. The larger the interline space, the more pronounced the line rhythm.

Text with progressive interline space.

Column two
Line length rhythm.
Justified text with monotonous rhythm.

Ragged text with a lively rhythm.

Strong rhythm determined by the syntax structure of the text. The extreme difference of line lengths interferes with legibility.

Rhythm determined by word length.

Line rhythm

Interline space is the rhythmic unit of text. It determines the distance from baseline to baseline, how close or how far apart the individual lines appear. The larger the interline space, the coarser the rhythm and the fewer the number of lines that can fit in a given space.

The rhythm of text set solid is very different from the same text set with increased interline space. In a text set solid, the individual lines are unobtrusive, appearing as a single mass. In text set with interline space, each line is more pronounced. The expression of the text changes depending on its rhythm.

In justified text, the right hand edge lacks rhythm. In ragged text, the alternating short and long lines create a lively rhythm. Depending on the intended effect, the line rhythm may be subtle or pronounced.

Twenty-three miles from Agra in India, wi
th its fabled Taj Mahal, lies Fatepur Sikri,
a dream city built in sandstone the colors
of the dying sunset. One approaches Fate
pur Sikri in silence, for it has been desert
ed for over two hundred years, but imme
diately on entering the core of the city, th
e Mahal-i-Khas, the heart is uplifted, the e
ye entranced. One experiences a rare sen
sation of freedom and repose, an invitati
on to step forward buoyantly and, at the
same time, to loiter luxuriously. Wherever
the eye turns the view is held, but at ever
y step it changes. A seemingly solid back
ground wall of stone is later perceived as

Twenty-three miles from Agra in India, wi
th its fabled Taj Mahal, lies Fatepur Sikri,
a dream city built in sandstone the colors
of the dying sunset. One approaches Fate
pur Sikri in silence, for it has been desert

diately on entering the core of the city, th
e Mahal-i-Khas, the heart is uplifted, the e
ye entranced. One experiences a rare sen
sation of freedom and repose, an invitati
on to step forward buoyantly and, at the
same time, to loiter luxuriously. Wherever
the eye turns the view is held, but at ever
y step it changes. A seemingly solid back
ground wall of stone is later perceived as

Twenty-three miles from Agra in India, wi
th its fabled Taj Mahal, lies Fatepur Sikri,
a dream city built in sandstone the colors
of the dying sunset. One approaches Fate
pur Sikri in silence, for it has been desert

e Mahal-i-Khas, the heart is uplifted, the e
ye entranced. One experiences a rare sen
sation of freedom and repose, an invitati
on to step forward buoyantly and, at the
same time, to loiter luxuriously. Wherever
the eye turns the view is held, but at ever
y step it changes. A seemingly solid back
ground wall of stone is later perceived as

Twenty-three miles from Agra in India, wi
th its fabled Taj Mahal, lies Fatepur Sikri,
a dream city built in sandstone the colors
of the dying sunset. One approaches Fate
pur Sikri in silence, for it has been desert

ye entranced. One experiences a rare sen
sation of freedom and repose, an invitati
on to step forward buoyantly and, at the
same time, to loiter luxuriously. Wherever
the eye turns the view is held, but at ever
y step it changes. A seemingly solid back
ground wall of stone is later perceived as

Twenty-three miles from Agra in India, wi
th its fabled Taj Mahal, lies Fatepur Sikri,
a dream city built in sandstone the colors
of the dying sunset. One approaches Fate
pur Sikri in silence, for it has been desert
ed for over two hundred years, but imme
diately on entering the core of the city, th
e Mahal-i-Khas, the heart is uplifted, the e

The Moving Eye
on to step forward buoyantly and, at the
same time, to loiter luxuriously. Wherever
the eye turns the view is held, but at ever
y step it changes. A seemingly solid back
ground wall of stone is later perceived as

Twenty-three miles from Agra in India, wi
th its fabled Taj Mahal, lies Fatepur Sikri,
a dream city built in sandstone the colors
of the dying sunset. One approaches Fate
pur Sikri in silence, for it has been desert
ed for over two hundred years, but imme
diately on entering the core of the city, th

The Moving Eye

on to step forward buoyantly and, at the
same time, to loiter luxuriously. Wherever
the eye turns the view is held, but at ever
y step it changes. A seemingly solid back
ground wall of stone is later perceived as

Twenty-three miles from Agra in India, wi
th its fabled Taj Mahal, lies Fatepur Sikri,
a dream city built in sandstone the colors
of the dying sunset. One approaches Fate
pur Sikri in silence, for it has been desert
ed for over two hundred years, but imme

The Moving Eye

on to step forward buoyantly and, at the
same time, to loiter luxuriously. Wherever
the eye turns the view is held, but at ever
y step it changes. A seemingly solid back
ground wall of stone is later perceived as

Twenty-three miles from Agra in India, wi
th its fabled Taj Mahal, lies Fatepur Sikri,
a dream city built in sandstone the colors
of the dying sunset. One approaches Fate
pur Sikri in silence, for it has been desert
ed for over two hundred years, but imme

Agra

on to step forward buoyantly and, at the
same time, to loiter luxuriously. Wherever
the eye turns the view is held, but at ever
y step it changes. A seemingly solid back
ground wall of stone is later perceived as

Twenty-three miles from Agra in India, wi
th its fabled Taj Mahal, lies Fatepur Sikri,
a dream city built in sandstone the colors
of the dying sunset. One approaches Fate

pur Sikri in silence, for it has been desert
ed for over two hundred years, but imme
diately on entering the core of the city, th
e Mahal-i-Khas, the heart is uplifted, the e
ye entranced. One experiences a rare sen

sation of freedom and repose, an invitati
on to step forward buoyantly and, at the
same time, to loiter luxuriously. Wherever
the eye turns the view is held, but at ever
y step it changes. A seemingly solid back

Column one
The line rhythm of text. The line rhythm interrupted by one, two, and three blank lines. The overall rhythm is maintained.

Column two
Subtitles placed in two, three, and four line spaces. The overall rhythm is interrupted by the subtitle.

Column three
Arbitrary space between paragraphs destroys the line rhythm.

Paragraph rhythm

For legibility and readability, text is divided into paragraphs. The individual paragraphs are marked by indenting or extending the first line, or by inserting a full line space. These methods of delineating a paragraph maintain the text's line rhythm.

Extra space for titles, subtitles, quotations, and illustrations should be a multiple of the established interline space to maintain line rhythm. If the main text is set in 9/11 point type, that is 9 point type with 11 point interline space, all horizontal spaces in the text should be a multiple of 11 point, for instance 22, 33, or 44 point.

Within that space, a subtitle is placed with more space above than below. The total space, including the element placed within it, is equivalent to a multiple of the established interline space.

Jean Prouvé
Three Nomadic Structures
April 12–May 10
Arthur Ross Gallery
Buell Hall
Columbia University
New York City

Jean Prouvé

Three Nomadic Structures

April 12–May 10

Arthur Ross Gallery

Buell Hall

Columbia University

New York City

Jean Prouvé
Three Nomadic Structures

April 12–May 10

Arthur Ross Gallery
Buell Hall
Columbia University
New York City

Jean Prouvé
Three Nomadic Structures

April 12–May 10

Arthur Ross Gallery
Buell Hall

Columbia University
New York City

Jean Prouvé
Three Nomadic Structures

April 12–May 10
Arthur Ross Gallery
Buell Hall
Columbia University
New York City

Jean Prouvé
Three Nomadic Structures

April 12–May 10
Arthur Ross Gallery
Buell Hall
Columbia University
New York City

Jean Prouvé
Three Nomadic Structures

April 12–May 10
Arthur Ross Gallery
Buell Hall
Columbia University
New York City

Jean Prouvé
Three Nomadic Structures

April 12–May 10

Arthur Ross Gallery
Buell Hall

Columbia University
New York City

Column one
Frame one: line lengths establish the rhythm.

Frame two: uniform interline space creates a monotonous rhythm.

Frames three and four: line groups and spacing create an animated rhythm.

Column two
Horizontal line shifts create an additional rhythm.

Typographic information consisting of seven lines.
The rhythm is altered by increasing the interline space, and clustering and shifting the lines. Changes of line space noticeably affect the text's rhythm.

Through change of typesize, weight, width, and slant, additional variations in rhythm can be created. However, the more variations that are introduced the more ambiguous the rhythm. An effective rhythm is easy to discern.

Twenty-three miles from Agra in India, with its fabled Taj Mahal, lies Fatepur Sikri, a dream city built in sandstone the colors of the dying sunset.

One approaches Fatepur Sikri in silence, for it has been deserted for over two hundred years, but immediately on entering the core of the city, the Mahal-i-Khas, the heart is uplifted, the eye entranced.

One experiences a rare sensation of freedom and repose, an invitation to step forward buoyantly and, at the same time, to loiter luxuriously.

Wherever the eye turns the view is held, but at every step it changes. A seemingly solid background wall of stone is later perceived as a transparent screen.

But nowhere is there a fixed center: nowhere a point from which the observer can dominate the whole. Equally nowhere does he stand conspicuously removed from the center, a spectator in the wings.

From the moment he steps within this urban core he becomes an intimate part of the scene, which does not impose itself upon him, but discloses itself gradually to him, at his own pace and according to his own pleasure.

Structured rhythm with six text blocks.

Free rhythm with six text blocks.

Stepped rhythm with three different size text blocks.

Twenty-three miles from Agra in India, with its fabled Taj Mahal, lies Fatepur Sikri, a dream city built in sandstone the colors of the dying sunset.

One approaches Fatepur Sikri in silence, for it has been deserted for over two hundred years, but immediately on entering the core of the city, the Mahal-i-Khas, the heart is uplifted, the eye entranced.

But nowhere is there a fixed center: nowhere a point from which the observer can dominate the whole. Equally nowhere does he stand conspicuously removed from the center, a spectator in the wings.

From the moment he steps within this urban core he becomes an intimate part of the scene, which does not impose itself upon him, but discloses itself gradually to him, at his own pace and according to his own pleasure.

One experiences a rare sensation of freedom and repose, an invitation to step forward buoyantly and, at the same time, to loiter luxuriously.

Wherever the eye turns the view is held, but at every step it changes. A seemingly solid background wall of stone is later perceived as a transparent screen.

Twenty-three miles from Agra in India, with its fabled Taj Mahal, lies Fatepur Sikri, a dream city built in sandstone the colors of the dying sunset. One approaches Fatepur Sikri in silence, for it has been deserted for over two hundred years, but immediately on entering the core of the city, the Mahal-i-Khas, the heart is uplifted, the eye entranced.

One experiences a rare sensation of freedom and repose, an invitation to step forward buoyantly and, at the same time, to loiter luxuriously. Wherever the eye turns the view is held, but at every step it changes. A seemingly solid background wall of stone is later perceived as a transparent screen. But nowhere is there a fixed center: nowhere a point from which the observer can dominate the whole. Equally nowhere does he stand conspicuously removed from the center, a spectator in the wings. From the moment he steps within this urban core he becomes an intimate part of the

scene, which does not impose itself upon him, but discloses itself gradually to him, at his own pace and according to his own pleasure. The Mahal-i-Khas was the core of a city of perhaps fifty thousand people. It is a place somewhat larger than the Piazza San Marco in Venice.

20:00

Buttons
have been
left for stones
Pierced through
we save them
for
tomorrow

But find
instead
at eight o'clock
a piece of glass
run smooth
by water
will do as well

And since
it isn't
as familiar
as buttons
we will
save it as
talisman
to our
disorder

David Shapiro: Five Series

Paintings
Drawings
Prints

Fort Wayne Museum of Art, Fort Wayne, IN   September 3 - October 3   **1982**

Butler Institute of American Art, Youngstown, OH   November 7 - November 28   **1982**

Canton Art Institute, Canton, OH   January 16 - February 13   **1982**

Columbia University
Graduate School of Architecture
Planning and Preservation

L I M E W O R K S : **Photography by Naoya Hatakeyama**

Exhibition
March 6–May 1
400 Avery Hall
116 Street/Broadway

Page from a poetry book. The stepped rhythm of the poetry contrasts with the static rectangular photograph.

Exhibit announcement. The rhythm of exhibit title contrasts with the artist's name.

Title page for an exhibit catalog. Contrasting rhythms are created by vertical and horizontal typographic lines of different lengths.

	J	F	**M**	A	M	**J**	J	A	**S**	O	N	**D**
M									1			1
T				1			1		2			2
W	1			2			2		3	1		3
T	2			3	1		3		4	2		4
F	3			4	2		4	1	5	3		5
S	4	1	1	5	3		5	2	6	4	1	6
S	5	2	2	6	4	1	6	3	7	5	2	7
M	6	3	3	7	5	2	7	4	8	6	3	8
T	7	4	4	8	6	3	8	5	9	7	4	9
W	8	5	5	9	7	4	9	6	10	8	5	10
T	9	6	6	10	8	5	10	7	11	9	6	11
F	10	7	7	11	9	6	11	8	12	10	7	12
S	11	8	8	12	10	7	12	9	13	11	8	13
S	12	9	9	13	11	8	13	10	14	12	9	14
M	13	10	10	14	12	9	14	11	15	13	10	15
T	14	11	11	15	13	10	15	12	16	14	11	16
W	15	12	12	16	14	11	16	13	17	15	12	17
T	16	13	13	17	15	12	17	14	18	16	13	18
F	17	14	14	18	16	13	18	15	19	17	14	19
S	18	15	15	19	17	14	19	16	20	18	15	20
S	19	16	16	20	18	15	20	17	21	19	16	21
M	20	17	17	21	19	16	21	18	22	20	17	22
T	21	18	18	22	20	17	22	19	23	21	18	23
W	22	19	19	23	21	18	23	20	24	22	19	24
T	23	20	20	24	22	19	24	21	25	23	20	25
F	24	21	21	25	23	20	25	22	26	24	21	26
S	25	22	22	26	24	21	26	23	27	25	22	27
S	26	23	23	27	25	22	27	24	28	26	23	28
M	27	24	24	28	26	23	28	25	29	27	24	29
T	28	25	25	29	27	24	29	26	30	28	25	30
W	29	26	26	30	28	25	30	27		29	26	31
T	30	27	27		29	26	31	28		30	27	
F	31	28	28		30	27		29		31	28	
S			29		31	28		30			29	
S			30			29		31			30	
M			31			30						
T												
W												
T												
F												
S												
S												

be inspired **2003**

Columbia University
Graduate School of Architecture
Planning and Preservation

Thursday,
February 28
1:00pm

Wood Auditorium
Avery Hall

Tadao Ando

Recent work

●　●

●　●

Lecture invitation. Contrast between the rhythm of the four elements of typographic information and the four dots.

Season's greetings card. Strong rhythm created by the days and months of the calendar matrix.

Lecture with slides

Tuesday
May 6, 3:00 pm
Room 276

Basic Design Education

Manfred Maier
Professor of Graphic Design
Allgemeine Gewerbeschule (School of Design) Basel, Switzerland

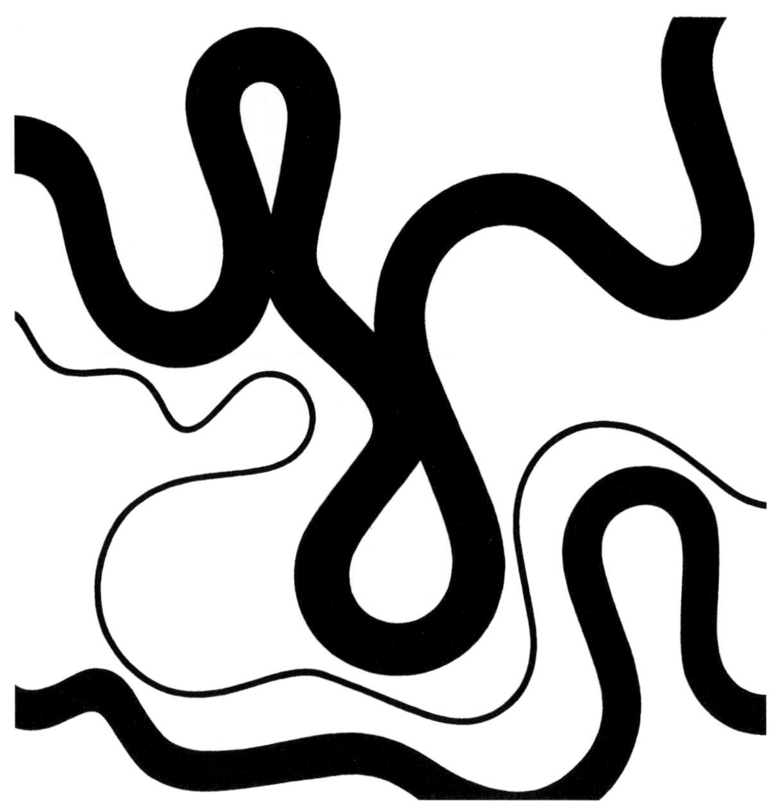

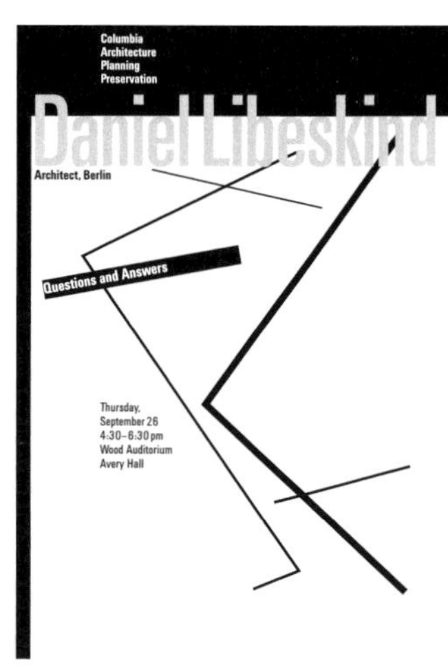

Lecture poster. Contrast between the strong rhythm of the graphic illustration and the typography structure.

Lecture invitation. Contrast between the rhythm of angular line elements and the typography.

DESIGNER'S SATURDAY
The Center of Design
NEW YORK
OCTOBER 6 7 8

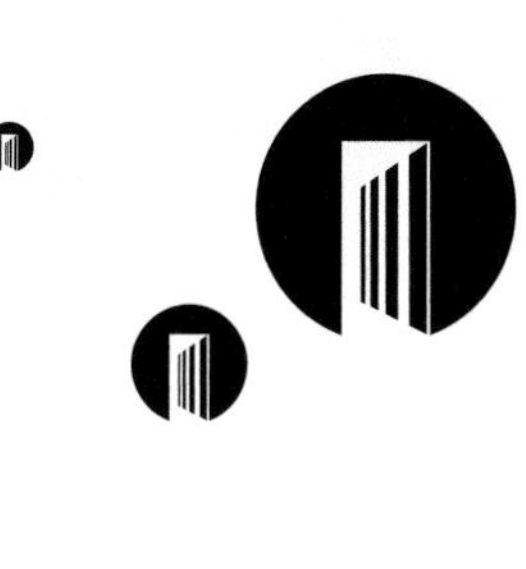

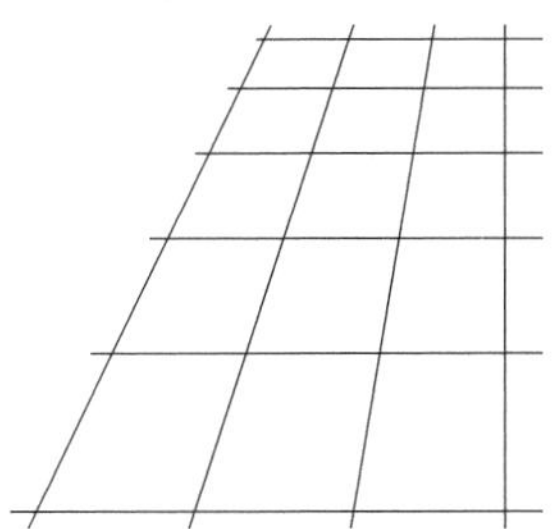

OCTOBER 6 7 8

Designer's Saturday poster. The design combines five different rhythms: the rhythm of the three symbols; the rhythm of the three lines of event information; the rhythm of the linear grid; the rhythm of the dates; and the rhythm of the cloud formation.

The symbol's 'open door' rhythm complements the poster's design rhythm.

Buell Evening Lecture
co-sponsored by
Skidmore, Owings & Merrill

Friday, April 19

Toyo Ito
Architect, Japan

Recent work

Lecture series poster. The design is based on a strong vertical rhythm of lectures, symposia, and exhibitions.

Detail of line rhythm on the microaesthetic level.

Diagram of conceptual framework.

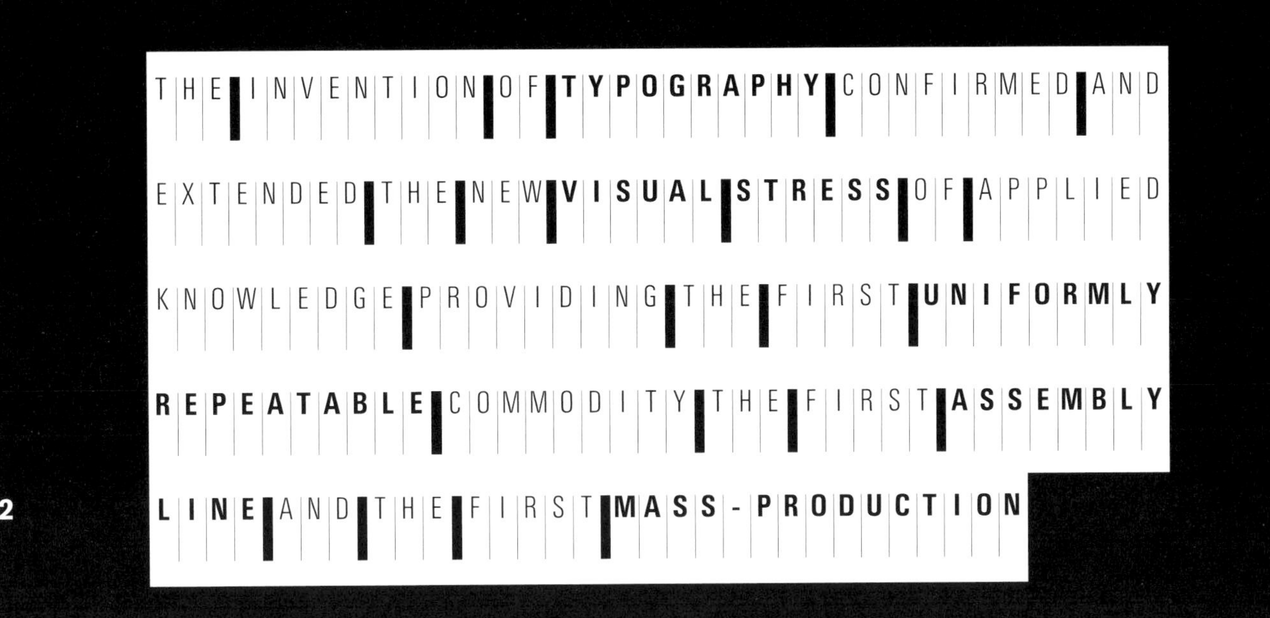

12
THE INVENTION OF TYPOGRAPHY CONFIRMED AND
EXTENDED THE NEW VISUAL STRESS OF APPLIED
KNOWLEDGE PROVIDING THE FIRST UNIFORMLY
REPEATABLE COMMODITY THE FIRST ASSEMBLY
LINE AND THE FIRST MASS-PRODUCTION

Typographic interpretation of a quote by Marshall McLuhan. The design combines two different rhythms: the rhythm of bold and light vertical lines deriving from word and letter space, and the rhythm of the bold and light letters.

The design expresses the concept of visual stress, uniformly repeatable, assembly line, and mass-production.

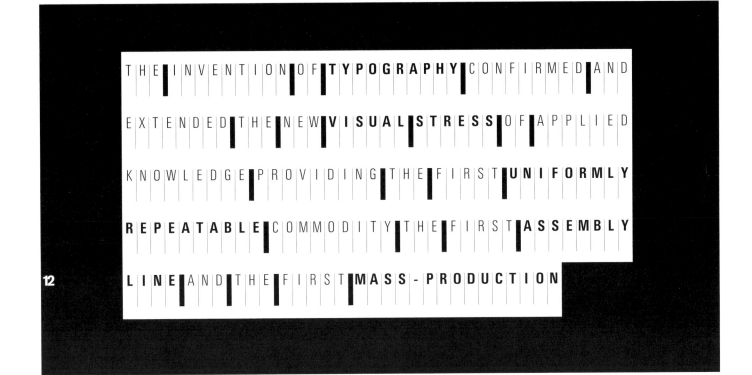

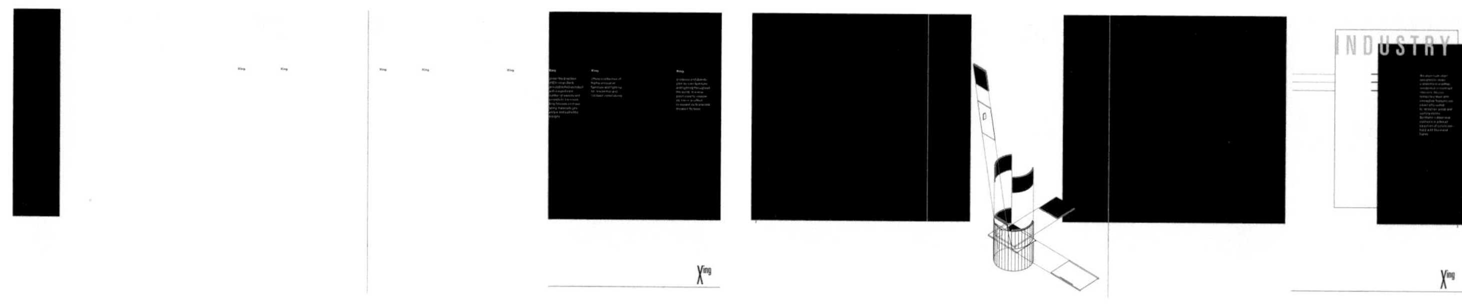

Catalog for a furniture designer. Conceptual idea: to present the products in a syncopated rhythm, similar to a filmstrip.

Concept of brochure rhythm.

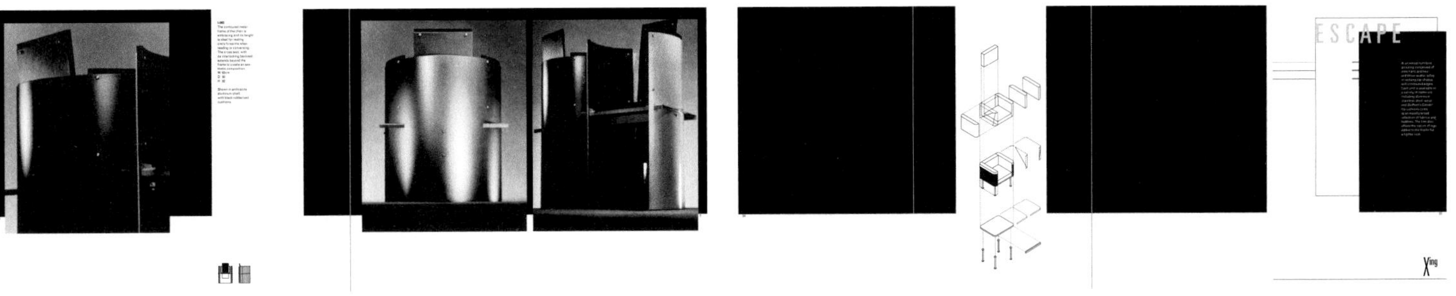

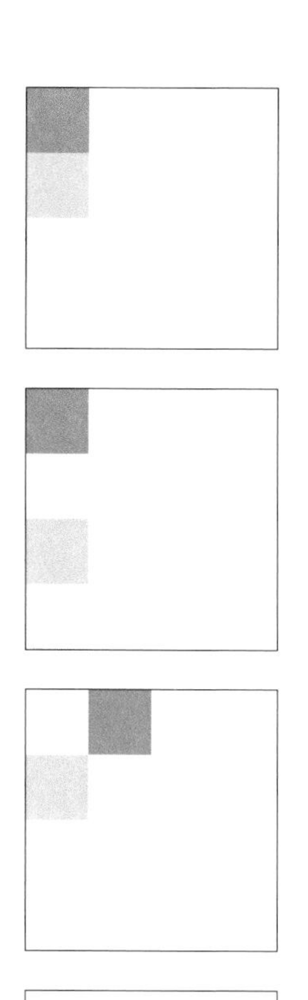

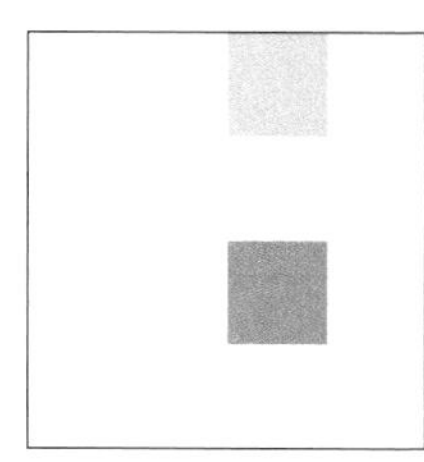
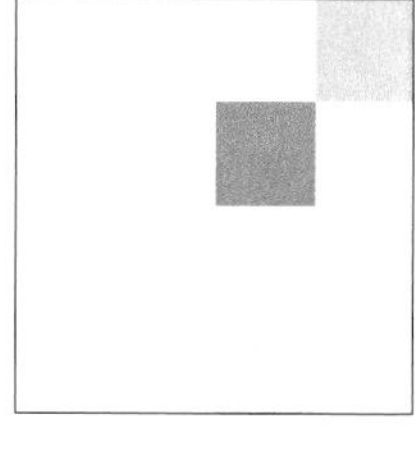

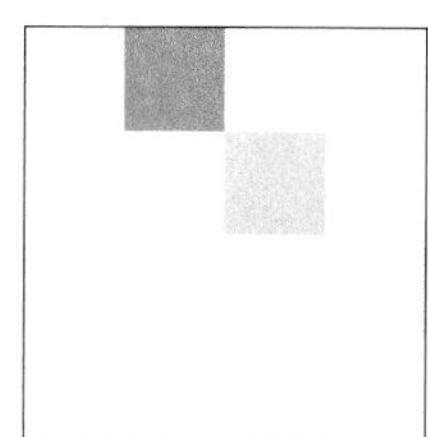

Compositions with three gray squares representing typographic information. Although each composition has the same elements, each has a different expression.

Column one
Frame one: squares stacked with minimal visual effect.

Frame two: squares composed with some visual effect.

Frames three to five: squares composed within two columns; moderate visual effect.

Column two
Squares composed within two columns: moderate visual effect.

Column three
Squares composed within three columns: strong visual effect.

Composition

The composition of typographic elements is the essence of design. The way the elements are arranged determines both the content and the form of information. In other words, the composition articulates the information. Without a clear composition, information is daunting and lacks the visual cues to catch the reader's attention.

The typographic designer must understand how best to arrange the visual units to make information accessible and comprehensible to the reader. Just as a series of words can be composed in different ways to form a sentence, components of information can be arranged in many configurations to convey the information. Although the various compositions may convey the same meaning, each evokes a different emotional response.

Divided into smaller units, typographic information becomes more focused and invites closer inspection. The more the information is 'atomized' – that is, dissected into smaller units – the more possibilities for compositions emerge. However, because the objective of typographic design is to optimize information, the question then becomes: how much can information be atomized without affecting legibility?

Biography
1907 Born in Engelberg, Switzerland
1925-27 Studied painting at the École des Beaux-Arts, Geneva
1928-29 Studied at the Académie Moderne in Paris
under Fernand Léger and Ozenfant
Became interested in photography and design
1929-32 Still in Paris, worked with AM Cassandre on posters,
with Le Corbusier on architecture and exhibitions
and with Deberny & Peignot as a photographer and typographer
1932-36 Returned to Zürich and designed the poster series
for the Swiss National Tourist Office
1936 Came to the United States
Worked as freelance photographer for *Harpers Bazaar*,
Vogue and other magazines
1946-66 Design consultant for Knoll Associates Inc
1949 Produced the color film *Works of Calder* (MoMA)
1952-76 Professor of photography, Yale University
1954-55 Comprehensive design program for the New Haven Railroad
1958-68 Design consultant for the Solomon R Guggenheim Museum
and the Museum of Fine Arts, Houston
1960-77 Photographed the work of Alberto Giacometti
1984 Dies in Southampton, New York

Biography

1907	Born in Engelberg, Switzerland
1925-27	Studied painting at the École des Beaux-Arts, Geneva
1928-29	Studied at the Académie Moderne in Paris
	under Fernand Léger and Ozenfant
	Became interested in photography and design
1929-32	Still in Paris, worked with AM Cassandre on posters,
	with Le Corbusier on architecture and exhibitions
	and with Deberny & Peignot as a photographer and typographer
1932-36	Returned to Zürich and designed the poster series
	for the Swiss National Tourist Office
1936	Came to the United States
	Worked as freelance photographer for *Harpers Bazaar*,
	Vogue and other magazines
1946-66	Design consultant for Knoll Associates Inc
1949	Produced the color film *Works of Calder* (MoMA)
1952-76	Professor of photography, Yale University
1954-55	Comprehensive design program for the New Haven Railroad
1958-68	Design consultant for the Solomon R Guggenheim Museum
	and the Museum of Fine Arts, Houston
1960-77	Photographed the work of Alberto Giacometti
1984	Dies in Southampton, New York

Biography

Born in Engelberg, Switzerland	1907
Studied painting at the École des Beaux-Arts, Geneva	1925-27
Studied at the Académie Moderne in Paris	1928-29
under Fernand Léger and Ozenfant	
Became interested in photography and design	
Still in Paris, worked with AM Cassandre on posters,	1929-32
with Le Corbusier on architecture and exhibitions	
and with Deberny & Peignot as a photographer and typographer	
Returned to Zürich and designed the poster series	1932-36
for the Swiss National Tourist Office	
Came to the United States	1936
Worked as freelance photographer for *Harpers Bazaar*,	
Vogue and other magazines	
Design consultant for Knoll Associates Inc	1946-66
Produced the color film *Works of Calder* (MoMA)	1949
Professor of photography, Yale University	1952-76
Comprehensive design program for the New Haven Railroad	1954-55
Design consultant for the Solomon R Guggenheim Museum	1958-68
and the Museum of Fine Arts, Houston	
Photographed the work of Alberto Giacometti	1960-77
Dies in Southampton, New York	1984

A certain structure is inherent in all typographic information. Discovering and working with this structure leads to different compositions.

Three examples of information transformed into different typographic compositions.
Frame one contains the raw information.
Frames two and three: logical separation of the typographic information creates different compositions.

Contents
Introduction 3
History of the Graduate School 4
Faculty 6
Core Architecture Studios 8
Studio 1 10
Studio 2 18
Studio 3 26
Advanced Architecture Studios 34
Studio 4 36
Studio 5 44
Studio 6 58
MS Advanced Architectural Design 74
MS Architecture and Urban Design 82
GSAP Computer Sequence 90
Building Technologies 98
History/Theory 110
Architectural Drawing I, II 112
MS Urban Planning 114
MS Historic Preservation 122
Real Estate Development 126
The Shape of Two Cities: New York-Paris 128
Barnard/Columbia Undergraduate 132
Buell Center for the Study of American Architecture 138
Columbia Research Centers 140
Avery Library 141
Office of Publications 142
Foreign Travel and Study Programs 144
Awards and Fellowships 147
Architecture Galleries 148
Lectures and Symposia 150
Year-End Exhibition 158
Final Design Studio Juries 160

Contents		
	Introduction	3
	History of the Graduate School	4
	Faculty	6
	Core Architecture Studios	8
	Studio 1	10
	Studio 2	18
	Studio 3	26
	Advanced Architecture Studios	34
	Studio 4	36
	Studio 5	44
	Studio 6	58
	MS Advanced Architectural Design	74
	MS Architecture and Urban Design	82
	GSAP Computer Sequence	90
	Building Technologies	98
	History/Theory	110
	Architectural Drawing I, II	112
	MS Urban Planning	114
	MS Historic Preservation	122
	Real Estate Development	126
	The Shape of Two Cities: New York-Paris	128
	Barnard/Columbia Undergraduate	132
	Buell Center for the Study of American Architecture	138
	Columbia Research Centers	140
	Avery Library	141
	Office of Publications	142
	Foreign Travel and Study Programs	144
	Awards and Fellowships 1999	147
	Architecture Galleries	148
	Lectures and Symposia	150
	Year-End Exhibition	158
	Final Design Studio Juries	160

Contents		
	3	Introduction
	4	History of the Graduate School
	6	Faculty
	8	Core Architecture Studios
	10	Studio 1
	18	Studio 2
	26	Studio 3
	34	Advanced Architecture Studios
	36	Studio 4
	44	Studio 5
	58	Studio 6
	74	MS Advanced Architectural Design
	82	MS Architecture and Urban Design
	90	GSAP Computer Sequence
	98	Building Technologies
	110	History/Theory
	112	Architectural Drawing I, II
	114	MS Urban Planning
	122	MS Historic Preservation
	126	Real Estate Development
	128	The Shape of Two Cities: New York-Paris
	132	Barnard/Columbia Undergraduate
	138	Buell Center for the Study of American Architecture
	140	Columbia Research Centers
	141	Avery Library
	142	Office of Publications
	144	Foreign Travel and Study Programs
	147	Awards and Fellowships 1999
	148	Architecture Galleries
	150	Lectures and Symposia
	158	Year-End Exhibition
	160	Final Design Studio Juries

February
19 Siza
26 Tschumi
March
05 SOM
07 Berman
12 Richter
24 Wilson
26 Koolhaas
April
02 Lavin
16 Teyssot
23 Holl

February

19	Siza
26	Tschumi

March

05	SOM
07	Berman
12	Richter
24	Wilson
26	Koolhaas

April

02	Lavin
16	Teyssot
23	Holl

February	19	Siza
	26	Tschumi
March	05	SOM
	07	Berman
	12	Richter
	24	Wilson
	26	Koolhaas
April	02	Lavin
	16	Teyssot
	23	Holl

Typography has many intrinsic forms – for instance, the form of a word, a sentence, a text, a quotation, a poem, or a list. The form of a text is intrinsically different from that of a timetable. The composition of each may have many different forms as long as the form supports the information.

A typographic solution develops from the typography's intrinsic form; the designer cannot force the material into a preconceived shape. Typographic form and content are inextricably linked.

Column one
Frame one: Text for an exhibition announcement. Minimal differentiation between individual parts is achieved by line breaks.

Frames two to five: Information with moderate differentiation between individual parts. Simple visual composition subdivides the space.

Columns two and three Typographic information with strong differentiation between individual parts.

Notes on Almost Nothing:
Mies van der Rohe's
Haus Lange and Haus Esters
September 17–
October 22
Arthur Ross Gallery
Buell Hall
Columbia University

Notes on Almost Nothing:
Mies van der Rohe's
Haus Lange and Haus Esters

September 17–
October 22

Arthur Ross Gallery
Buell Hall
Columbia University

Notes on Almost Nothing:
Mies van der Rohe's
Haus Lange and Haus Esters

September 17–
October 22

Arthur Ross Gallery
Buell Hall
Columbia University

Notes on Almost Nothing:
Mies van der Rohe's
Haus Lange and Haus Esters

September 17– October 22
Arthur Ross Gallery Buell Hall Columbia University

Notes on Almost Nothing:
Mies van der Rohe's
Haus Lange and Haus Esters

September 17–
October 22

Arthur Ross Gallery
Buell Hall
Columbia University

Notes on Almost Nothing:
Mies van der Rohe's
Haus Lange and Haus Esters

September 17– October 22
Arthur Ross Gallery Buell Hall Columbia University

Notes on Almost Nothing:
Mies van der Rohe's
Haus Lange and Haus Esters

September 17– October 22
Arthur Ross Gallery Buell Hall Columbia University

Notes on Almost Nothing:
Mies van der Rohe's
Haus Lange and Haus Esters

September 17–
October 22

Arthur Ross Gallery
Buell Hall
Columbia University

Notes on Almost Nothing:

Mies van der Rohe's
Haus Lange
and Haus Esters

September 17–
October 22

Arthur Ross Gallery Buell Hall Columbia University

Notes on Almost Nothing: Mies van der Rohe's Haus Lange and Haus Esters

Arthur Ross Gallery Buell Hall Columbia University

September 17–
October 22

Notes on Almost Nothing:
Mies van der Rohe's
Haus Lange and Haus Esters

Arthur Ross Gallery Buell Hall Columbia University

September 17–
October 22

Notes on Almost Nothing:
Mies van der Rohe's
Haus Lange
and Haus Esters

September 17–
October 22

Arthur Ross Gallery
Buell Hall
Columbia University

Notes on Almost Nothing:
Mies van der Rohe's
Haus Lange and Haus Esters

September 17–
October 22

Arthur Ross Gallery
Buell Hall
Columbia University

Notes on Almost Nothing:
Mies van der Rohe's
Haus Lange
and Haus Esters

September 17 – October 22

Arthur Ross Gallery
Buell Hall
Columbia University

Notes on
Almost Nothing:
Mies van der Rohe's
Haus Lange
and Haus Esters

September 17
–October 22

Arthur Ross Gallery
Buell Hall
Columbia University

Although the form of information is partially determined by the structure of language and grammar, a simple text can be composed and organized in many different ways. Exploring the different arrangements of elements makes typographic design immensely fascinating.

There is a distinction between a typographic composition and a structure. A structure results from understanding and explicating the relationships among parts of information. In a chart, for instance, the underlying structure develops from the logical organization of the information – that is, from the relationship between the individual pieces of data. A composition, however, is a particular arrangement of typographic information. For example, a chart may be arranged in a number of different ways, without changing the data.

Likewise, a text may be composed in different configurations without changing the grammatical structure of the information. In a final analysis, a composition also has a structure and a structure is a form of composition.

By changing a composition, the visual expression of typographic information is transformed. With a small number of parts, many compositions can be created,

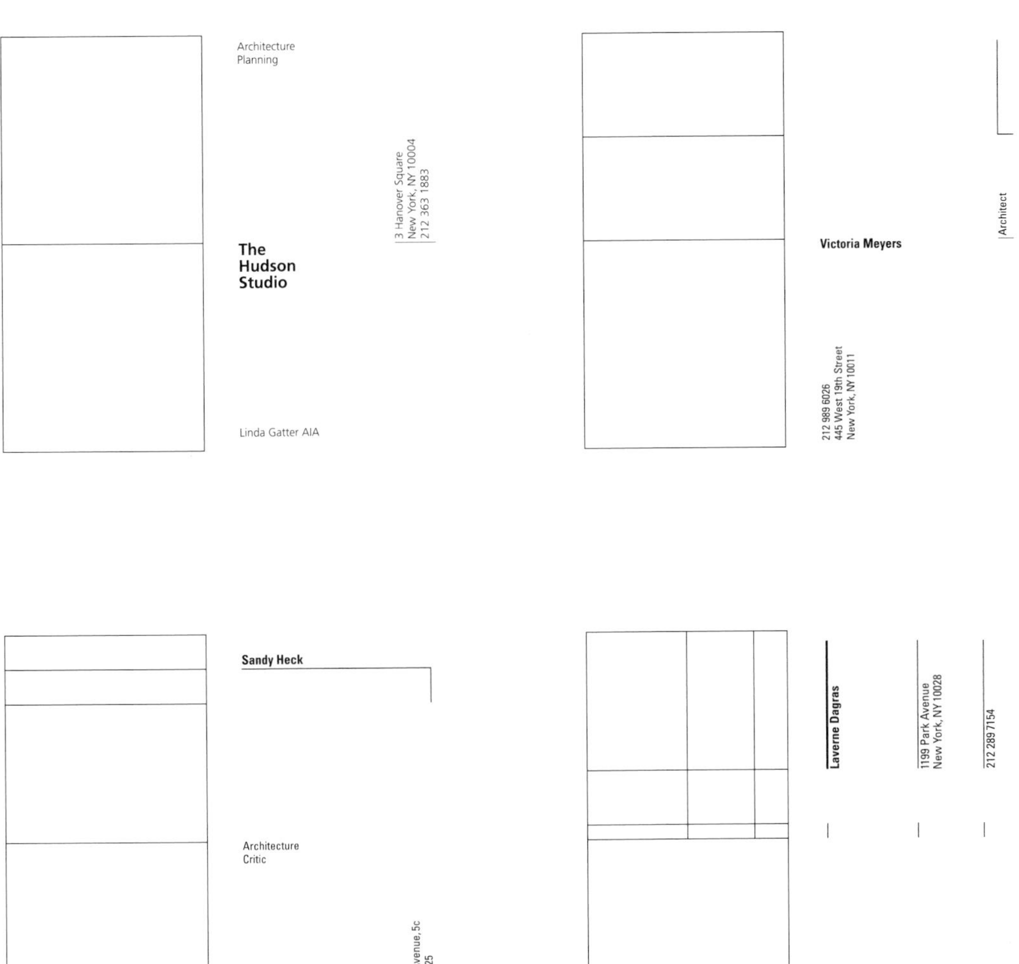

Four business cards based on a double square. The composition of typographic information is based on the mathematical subdivisions of the format.

each with its own visual expression. For instance, the composition can be rational, structured, random, playful, linear, stepped, tight, scattered, etc.

With a particular composition, the designer can semantically support the typographic information and increase legibility and readability.

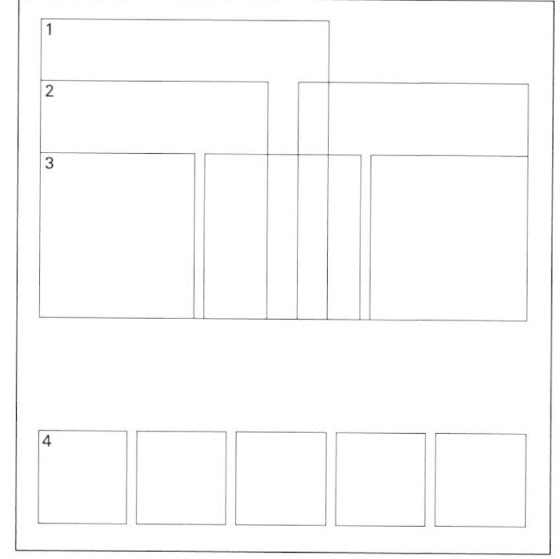

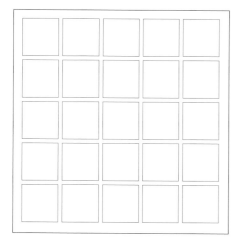

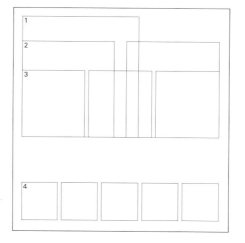

Column one
5x5 unit grid, developed after concept was established.

Grid with additional subdivisions for photographs.

Column two
Diagram of photograph sizes and placement.

Flow lines visible throughout the publication.

Design of the exhibition catalog for *New York the World's Premier Theater.* The composition originated with a visual concept.

Intended for a Japanese audience, the publication consists of five photographic essays with short introductions about important public spaces and events in New York City.

The visual concept of expressing the active rhythm of the city is reflected in the composition of square photographs in different sizes on each page. The composition adheres to three flow lines providing continuity throughout the publication.

Four typical double page spreads, starting with an introductory essay.

9x9 in.

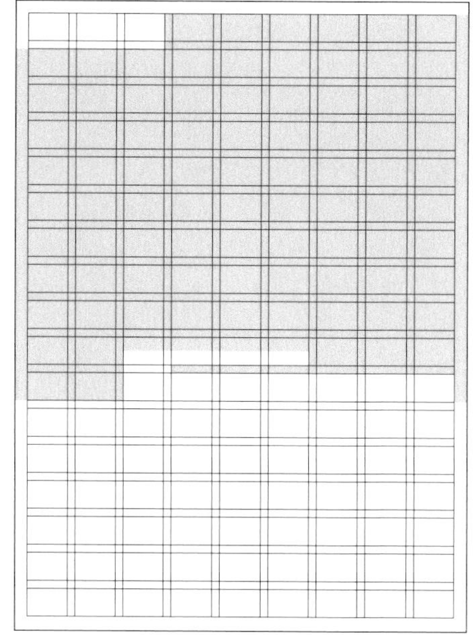

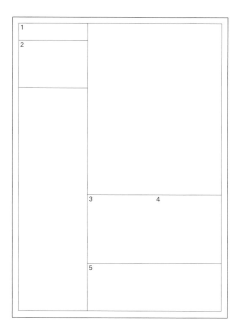

Composition based on typographic information. Zoning for the five components:
1 Date of events,
2 Title,
3 Text,
4 Annotations,
5 Captions.

A 9x17 unit grid determines the size and placement of photographs, captions, and text.

The gray field defines the primary illustration area and creates an additional optical level.

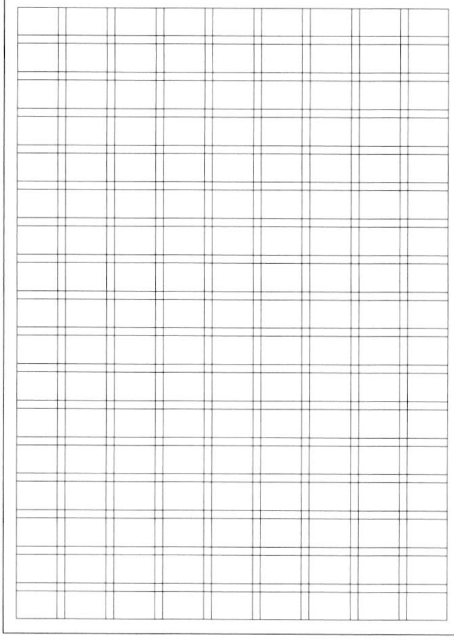

Design of the traveling exhibition *Nikken Sekkei, Its Ninety Years and the Modernization of Japan 1900–1989.*
The composition of each panel originated in the typographic information, which had five parts: date of events, title, text, annotations, and captions.

The finely detailed grid, consisting of 9x17 units, was developed after a careful study of the visual material and text to be featured on the 45 panels. The grid allows for the necessary variations in size and placement of photographs, captions, and text. The text is set on three, the annotations on two, and the captions on one grid unit.

The irregular gray field was introduced to define the primary illustration area and the placement of text on each panel. The field adds an optical level and creates strong continuity from panel to panel.

1935

Foreshadowing War: Osaka Stock Exchange

World War I did not not affect Japan, but she fought her own victorious war with Russia in 1905 and in 1931 invaded Manchuria. Emperor Meiji died in 1912 and Taisho in 1926.

While modernism and modern architecture with its 'International Style' were gaining footholds in Europe, the world-wide Great Depression of the late 1920s and early 1930s was slowly paving a road to militarization in both Europe and Japan.

At the same time, the raise of chauvinistic ideology and fascism was foreshadowing the outbreak of World War II, first in Europe and then in Japan.

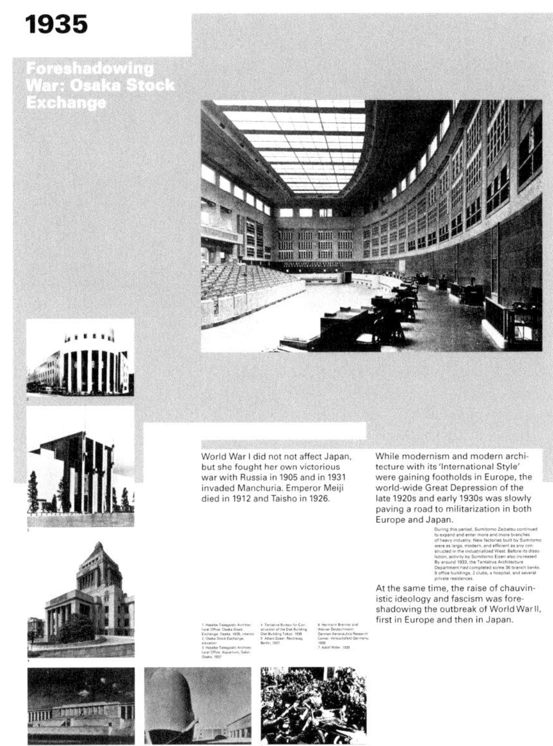

Fore
War

While m
tecture
were ga

During this peri
to expand and e
of heavy indust
were as large, n
structed in the i
lution, activity b

1 Hasebe-Takegos
tural Office: Osaka
Exchange, Osaka,
2 Osaka Stock Exc
elevation
3 Hasebe-Takegos
tural Office: Aquari

Typical panel
36x48 in.

Photographs and the interline space of the typography conform to the grid.

Microtypography.
There are two lines of title,
three lines of text,
six lines of annotated text,
or seven lines of caption
per grid unit.

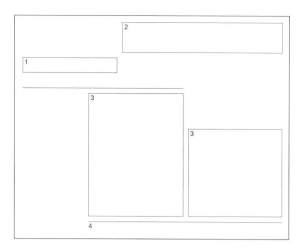

Composition based on typographic information. Information zones:
1 Title,
2 Competency statement,
3 Text,
4 Company identification.
Gray rectangular field unifies the typographic information and adds an optical level.

8x6 unit grid, developed after zoning was established.

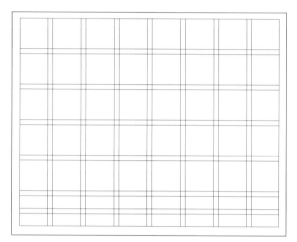

The composition of this capabilities brochure for a business-consulting firm was derived from the information that the firm wanted to convey. The information on each page consists of four parts: title, competency statement, text, and company identification.

The grid, consisting of eight columns and six rows, with the bottom row subdivided into half units, was developed after the hierarchy of typographic information on each page was established. All type sizes and interline space conform to the height of one grid unit (84 points) plus the space between units (14 points).

The gray 6x3 unit rectangular field unifies the typographic elements and adds an optical level to each page.

The competency statement is set five, the text three, and the company identification one column wide.

Presence

Azurian's Latin American network facilitates deployment of projects with both local sensitivity and regional scope and can bring expertise from several countries to a specific engagement.

Our regional network delivers the combined resources of seven offices. Miami has become the undisputed center of Latin American Internet activity and serves as the ideal point from which to establish our regional partnerships and spearhead our business development.

Our country offices are area nerve centers, staffed by consultants experienced in developing innovative solutions to the challenges of their own markets. Our teams are well positioned to form lasting partnerships with our clients, offering local expertise and Azurian's global quality standards.

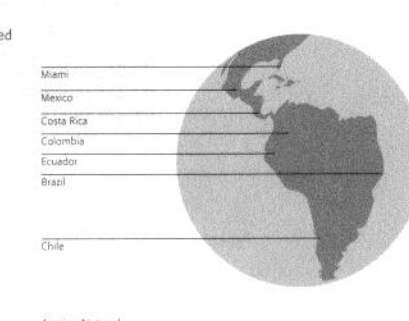

Azurian Network

2

Azurian

People

Azurian team members are selected for their regional expertise, Internet and industry experience and entrepreneurial attitude. They are led by an executive team of recognized change engineers with a passion for Internet business.

Azurian was founded by entrepreneurs who were passionate about bringing the power of the Internet to Latin America. Our entire team shares that energy and strives to implement e-business solutions that become revenue drivers for our clients.

Our exciting vision attracts high-caliber professionals to our strategic, creative and technology teams and our growing business provides the diverse challenges to keep them engaged. Career paths in the new economy are rarely straight and Azurian encourages its people to develop multidisciplinary skill sets and take on various roles in client engagements.

The Azurian environment is energized by individuals who are committed to growth and to putting our philosophy of continual improvement to work. This ambition is communicated to our clients who find both advisors and friends on their project teams.

The Azurian culture is a vibrant combination of all the cultures in which we work. Our project teams apply varied professional and national backgrounds, giving our clients the advantage of both a thorough local analysis and a global perspective.

Executive team

Our managers draw on many years of experience in different vertical and geographic markets and have achieved notable successes as technology entrepreneurs. Recognized for their ambition and initiative in Latin American Internet development, they have been tapped to discuss the Azurian vision at industry conferences from San Francisco to Santiago and have authored articles on e-business in prominent business publications in Colombia, Mexico and Central America. They are passionate about Azurian's goals and their excitement is transferred to each office and client relationship.

3

Azurian

Approach

Azurian solutions are tailored to the needs of each client business, designed to enhance performance and profitability, achieve competitive advantage and sustain market leadership.

Azurian projects are unique to each client but they share a common element – visible value creation. In addition to an expertly designed web presence that raises visibility in the marketplace and serves as a window into a business, our team develops business strategies and e-business applications that are focused on creating operational efficiencies and revenue streams.

We approach the challenges facing each business with an eIDEA. Azurian's eIDEA is a systematic, but flexible methodology that guides the development of our solutions to complex business problems. The process facilitates communication at crucial junctures, minimizes cost, time and risk for our clients and ensures quality and consistency in our deliverables.

Azurian eIDEA methodology

e	I	D	E	A
explore	Invent	Design	Execute	Advance
We discover unique business opportunities.	We envision e-business strategies that create value.	We create a detailed e-business blueprint.	We build and implement a comprehensive solution.	We extend the capabilities of the organization.

6

Azurian

Resources

Azurian's strategic software alliances, a reputed advisory board and the diverse backgrounds of our team members ensure that clients benefit from a broad talent base, thought leadership and leading edge technologies.

We build on our internal resources by continually incorporating the latest market developments into our operations. Our strategic alliances ensure that we offer our clients leading edge technologies and that our professionals receive the most current training in their applications.

In addition, we take full advantage of technologies that permit us to provide exemplary service and delivery. We encourage our clients to innovate to achieve market leadership and we implement the same philosophy in our own operations.

Advisory board

We leverage the knowledge of an impressive advisory board, comprised of thought leaders from respected Internet and new media firms. This unique panel of professionals lends its expertise in the new economy to our multi-faceted solutions.

Alliances

We have developed partnerships with the most respected Internet research groups and leading-edge technology vendors. We work with industry giants as well as new providers and are always looking for the newest and most agile solutions to bring to market.

We select our partners carefully. Our objectives are to find alliances and partnerships that provide key pieces of our end-to-end solutions and to stay ahead of new technology developments in the different areas of expertise. By aligning with many providers, we maintain the flexibility needed to bring the most appropriate solution to each client.

7

Azurian

Azurian teai
expertise, In
entrepreneu
team of recc

Our managers draw on
vertical and geographic
successes as technolog
ambition and initiative i
they have been tapped
industry conferences fr
authored articles on e-b

Typical double pages of the brochure. 11x8.5 in.

Microtypography. The type size and interline space of the competency statements and text conform to the height of one grid unit plus the space between units.

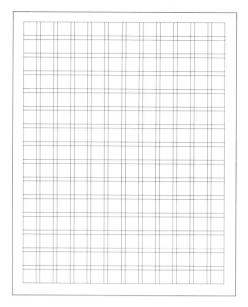

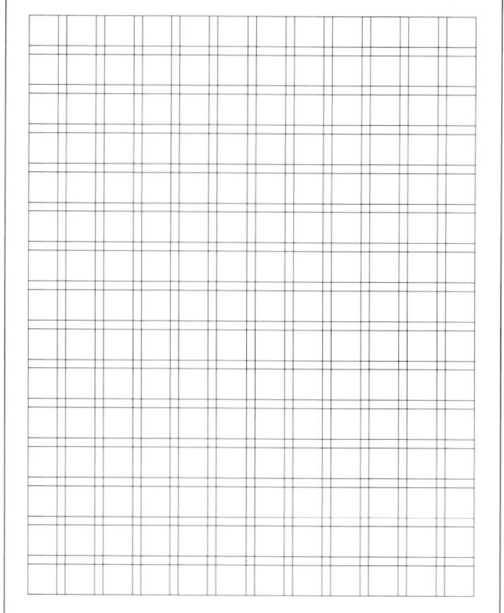

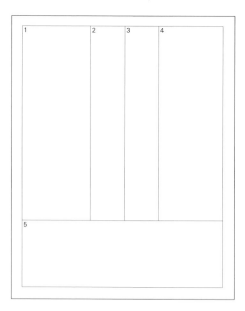

Zoning for the opening pages of the case studies. The information consists of:
1 Project title,
2 Subtitle,
3 Project data,
4 Illustrations,
5 Text.
On subsequent pages, illustrations and captions continue at the top of the page, with text at the bottom.

Zoning for technical essays. The information consists of:
1 Graphs and diagrams with captions,
2 Text.

12x15 unit modular grid for zones.

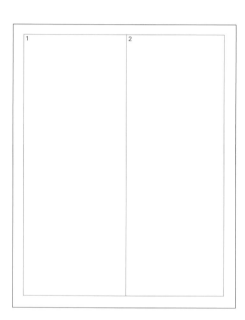

Design of the book *Sustainable Architecture in Japan: The Green Buildings of Nikken Sekkei.* The composition originated in the typographic information.

The publication consists of two parts, each with different typographic requirements: part one consists of ten case studies; part two contains eight technical essays on sustainable building design.

The 12x15 unit grid was developed after an in-depth study of the text and a diverse body of visual material including photographs, architectural drawings, graphs and diagrams. The grid allows for necessary variations in size and proportion of the visual materials. The macro-aesthetic details such as paragraph indents and hanging subtitles derive from the grid.

Part one is distinguished by a horizontal flow of images at the top and text at the bottom. The black field unifies the composition of images and supports the horizontal flow.

Part two uses a vertical flow of images on the left and text on the right of each page.

International Institute for Advanced Studies

1.1 The view from the patio of the Community Hall of the pond and research block.

The Grand Shoin Reinterpreted

The International Institute for Advanced Studies is Japan's first independent facility committed to futuristic research on a wide range of subjects. With participation of renowned scholars from around the world, intellectual inquiry at the Institute has ranged from a comparative study of happiness to molecular systematics. As a setting for high level scientific dialogue and investigation the built environment here is imbued with a pervasive tranquillity. Indeed, the calm, monastic atmosphere is among the many deliberate elements resulting from the institute's design. Nikken Sekkei approached the project as a respectful distillation of a pure, Japanese classical style that balances function and nature with the meditative space. Utilizing both modern and traditional materials and bio-safe technologies, the buildings and gardens of the IIAS pay unaffected homage to temple and shrine architecture from Kyoto and the surrounding district.

The Architectural Continuum and its Influences

IIAS is situated in an area of Kyoto Prefecture that is abundant with Japanese architectural history. The city flourished as the seat of the Japanese imperial court for over a thousand years, resulting in some of the finest architecture to be found in the Asiatic world. In 1994, UNESCO designated 17 regional buildings as World Cultural Heritage sites. A dominant thread running through these architectural expressions is the structure's harmonious relationship to its environment. Nature and its calming presence was adopted as a vital constituent of design evident in the highly mannered asceticism of houses, temples and gardens. Buildings from these periods defined living spaces freely through the use of open planned rooms, cypress bark roofs, wooden columns, wide, tiered verandahs, folding screens, tatami matting and deep eaves. Such temple and shrines are the reserves of many ancient building traditions and it's easy to see how the design of IIAS falls within the architectural continuum.

The arrival of Bhuddism in Japan had a lasting impact on the nation's architecture. In the periods that followed, the country moved away from outside influences to evolve a purely indigenous Japanese style shaped by the emergence of Zen, the Samurai culture, and the Shogunate. Bhuddist architecture built many teaching institutions throughout Japan where education and research was a sacred responsibility and Zen monasteries became sites of a constantly shifting guest population. Visiting priests, monks and novices alike were required to contribute their wisdom to the prevailing body of knowledge during their residency. The Togudo Hall of the Jishoji Temple (the Silver Pavilion) (1333–1573), is one of the finest expressions of the relationship between architecture and religion. It is the first built example of the "shoin-zukuri" or "grand shoin" form, a perfected style that would become the precursor of modern Japanese residential architecture. The primary word "shoin" is translated as "study hall", a place of learning and meditation.

Architecture as a Haven for the Mind

The "shoin" of IIAS has been called "a forum for agreeable contemplation and exchange." It consists of a residential-research complex named the "Scholar's Village" where visiting professors may conduct research and share their findings in candid debate in an open and totally supportive atmosphere. The Institute also has quiet, private spaces for reading, writing and just thinking.

The building site lies in a forested basin among the rolling hills of Keihanna, an area known for brilliant sunny days disrupted by high humidity, heavy rains and sudden mists. However, the consistent moisture factor endows the landscape with dazzling swathes of green, and causes a riotous blooming of cedar, cypress, cherry and ginko trees plus abundant flora indigenous to the area. (This weather pattern has long supported the flourishing of good timber for building materials in this region.)

The IIAS complex is generously positioned on the site using the traditional Ganko design, which produces a tiered or staggered construction. This form was chosen as a coping strategy against the

1.3

1.4

1.5

1.6

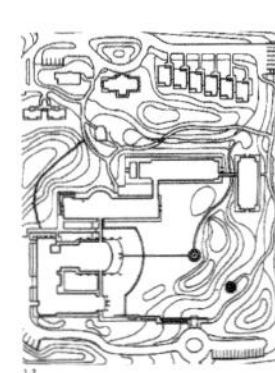

1.2

inconsistent weather and to facilitate easy contact among staff and researchers. The site plan establishes the principal building, with its deeply pitched roof, to the west with adjacent structures running on a long plane in a stepped sequence left of the central body. The main entrance is accessed via a circular drive protected from the nearby highway by a thick barrier of trees. All the build ings are low two floor structures with verandahs running the length of both facades. Wide eaves shield the balcony level, allowing the space to be used for human interaction and transit. The verandah space is reminiscent of early Japanese temple porches and serves to keep the interior cool and dry while allowing access to the exterior.

The landscaping scheme at the IIAS was designed to unify the exterior space between the building block and the surrounding terrain. Classically laid-out gardens providing serene vistas for the residents are displayed throughout the property. Banks of trees and flowering shrubs partially separate certain areas to create intimate, secluded groves and walkways. Man-made ponds and rivulets are strategically located as part of the consciously planned scenery. The ponds are constructed and positioned for their reflective qualities. The entire exterior surroundings are a successful orchestration designed to engender an aura of quietude and contemplation.

Bringing Nature Indoors

The interior design of the complex was conceived to maintain an aesthetic continuity with natural environment visible beyond the windows. The buildings comprise a community hall, a seminar lounge, administration offices, laboratories, a library, and a lecture theater. Each of the research laboratories provides a comfortable haven that allows for both work and relaxation. These rooms are basic but not austere and are equipped with desk units, sofas and spacious windows that permit the entry of gentle breezes. The simple doors and windows are sheltered with light screens that transform the sun into a soft unobtrusive light. The interior lighting is also muted and recessed above the seating and study areas. All of the labs open onto the gardens, permitting the residents to leave their desks to meet each other or to seek solitude for their thoughts.

The community hall in the main building functions as an informal communication space for guests and visitors. Its windows extend from the floor to the ceiling of the second level, allowing the entry of natural light for most of the day. The entrance has a curved frontage that opens on to an outdoor lounge with a spacious patio set before a still reflecting pond.

The seminar lounge of the research block has windows that are open to the garden on three sides, allowing for cross ventilation. Light-filtering screens shelter the expansive window units and smaller panes above them give a tranquil symmetry to the walls. The space is configured to adapt to academic debates, tutorial discussions and social gatherings.

Natural Ventilation Strategies to Combat Humidity

The periods of high humidity were a particular challenge to the Nikken Sekkei design team. It was essential that the living quarters provide visiting scholars with an agreeable temperature zone while utilizing natural air movement to aerate the buildings without have to resort to any artificial intervention or mechanical airflow systems. This dictated the use of large tiled roofs with deep eaves and wide window openings. Ensuring a cross breeze was essential; it is facilitated by the verandahs extending down either side of the dwelling units. The balcony on the second level is designed to cool the hot air near the windows. It too has the effect of encouraging through breezes. Covered connecting thru- ways between buildings are another defense against the heat, humidity and rain.

The architectural innovations incorporated into the design, that in ancient practice collaborated with the natural world to create buildings of harmony and grace, are proven at this site to still be as adaptable, durable and as enhancing to the environment as they were a thousand years ago.

Case studies, opening pages.

Case studies, typical double page.

9x12 in.

8

Sustainable Architecture: An East–West Perspective

Eiji Maki
Nikken Sekkei, Japan

and

William A. McDonough
William A. McDonough & Partners, USA

9

Eiji Maki

Architecture and Energy Saving

The vision and skill of the modern architect, no matter where they practice, essentially operates in a global context. The design of cities and buildings worldwide all contribute to the health or detriment of the earth's environment. Their environmental impact is not just localized, but extends across oceans, polar points and atmospheric layers. Given the inter-connections of these effects, it's the architect's primary responsibility to design buildings that are energy saving and protective of natural resources. This is an important principle at Nikken Sekkei and has been an integral part of our design protocols for many years. We have endeavored to achieve energy saving results by various design strategies, such as improving the envelope structure of buildings (utilizing outside stress shutoff by heat insulation and eaves) in the early stages of a project, and enhancing the efficiency of air-conditioning, lighting and load carriage in equipment planning.

Today, users of buildings, whether their habitat is the home or the work-space, require immediate comfort and convenience. This has led to an increased demand for energy in both the domestic and industrial sector, and we find ourselves in a situation where energy saving has never been so critical. Relevant regulations in Japan (such as PAL and CEC values) have become increasingly stringent. In order to implement permanent energy saving measures, it is crucial to determine and control the energy consumption in a building precisely. Technology for this purpose is also very important. However, energy-saving technologies in sustainable design is a constantly evolving process.

What is state-of-the art today is quickly subsumed by tomorrow's new innovations as we discover more refined solutions to energy conservation and environmental problems. Thus, we are required to constantly seek new and emerging technologies. One example is the use of power generation with solar heat; a system that reduces profligate consumption of energy resource by utilizing waste heat, waste-water and waste materials. Such technologies can be easily be utilized in sustainable design with very positive results. Over the years, I have closely followed the latest thinking on new and emerging technologies and have been able to integrate many new systems and materials into the design of several Nikken Sekkei buildings. I am positive that further progress will be made in innovative systems and new materials that save and recover energy.

Architecture and Global Environmental Problems

The concept of architecture existing in harmony with nature is not a new idea. Compelled by our industrial society's depredations against the environment, it's a mode of thinking about the design of building that we have been forced to revisit in Japan, (just as other architects have in other ecologically compromised regions). The amity between site and building, between the exterior wall and the forested perimeter is an ancient collaboration. Throughout the traditions of Japanese architecture, the function and form of buildings, from the lowliest woodcutter's hut to great temples, has always been meshed with the natural world. The modern notion of nature as an alien force that needs to be kept away from the built space, and even subjugated totally, is more a concept originating from industrial expansion. The elements were always allowed access in classical Japanese houses, gently channeled by simple, elegant design, whereby the building became an ally in the harnessed expressions of wind and sun. These spaces allowed the dweller to experience soft light filtered through shoji screens and cool breezes that traveled freely from porch to porch.

22

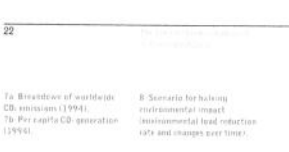

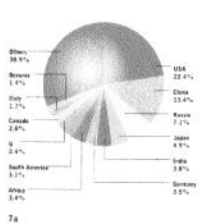

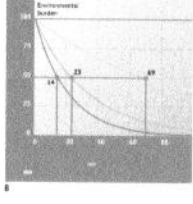

supplanted by uniform building designs predicated on the mass consumption of fossil fuels. Apart from the destruction that affects regional cultures on many levels, this approach is extraordinarily wasteful. A rough calculation of CO_2 generation in Japan (figure 9) indicates that 36% of Japan's CO_2 emissions are due to buildings, largely in the form of energy consumption. The three main types of energy consumption in buildings are air conditioning, lighting and conveyance, the movement of people, objects, air and water (figure 10). Buildings that generate a smaller environmental detriment are a key element in reducing total environmental impact. All those who create, own and maintain buildings have a great responsibility in this regard.

Can We Halve the Environmental Impact of Buildings?

Before we answer this question, we need some yardstick to quantify environmental impact. The most widely used indicator is Life Cycle CO_2 ($LCCO_2$). CO_2 is the major cause of global warming. $LCCO_2$ measures the environmental impact of a building over all the stages of its life, from the design through its demolition and disposal, in terms of the equivalent volume of CO_2 emission. igure 11 illustrates an example of a calculation for the $LCCO_2$ of a Japanese office building. It proves that the largest element in the building's $LCCO_2$ is the energy consumed in its operation. The environmental effects of construction and demolition are also substantial. Therefore the most important elements in $LCCO_2$ reduction are, in order:

1. Energy saving
2. Extending the life of the building
3. Use of eco-materials

Figure 11 shows the approximate $LCCO_2$ reduction per year that these three measures could yield. Halving the energy used in running the building would reduce $LCCO_2$ by approximately 30%. Extending the life of a building from 35 years to 100 years raises the $LCCO_2$ reduction to approximately 40%. The use of recycled materials such as blast-furnace cement could bring the $LCCO_2$ reduction to as much as 50%. Thus, there is a realistic prospect of reducing environmental impact by half.

Learning from Traditional Buildings

Traditional Japanese buildings offer superb examples of what we are trying to achieve in our buildings for the new century and the future. Their underlying principle is amity with the environment. They are close to nature and tailored to local conditions in ways that provide comfort with minimal energy consumption. Indigenous buildings in Japan that existed before the age of mass fossil energy consumption successfully minimized the environmental load, and were filled with elegant techniques for making use of natural energy. Such architecture avoids artificial uniformity, creating instead attractive and heterogeneous interior spaces and harmonious spatial relationships. These structures were designed to last and were built from renewable, locally available materials. We aim to learn the lessons offered by these superbly functional traditional buildings and apply them in our own green designs.

Buildings that exist harmoniously with nature have expression and forms that reflect the local land and climate. They also create delightful streets and towns. Traditional buildings are designed to arrive at a comfortable environmental balance through passive techniques. But the perception of comfort conditions in traditional buildings differs from modern perceptions. There was no intention of setting constant, arbitrary conditions of temperature and humidity. Neither was there any attempt to produce a constant, uniform lighting level. In traditional buildings, comfort was sought within acceptable ranges, with consideration being given to a comprehensive comfort including visual and aural aspects.

Component Technologies

The design principle embodied in traditional buildings, that they should regulate themselves to reach a comfortable environment without assistance, can be applied to the component technologies of a wide range of buildings.

Deep eaves or verandahs to block the sun's rays

The first step towards creating buildings which use natural energy is to prevent heat entering and to block sunlight. Japanese traditional buildings tend to emphasize sunlight blocking, while allowing air to pass through the structure.

23

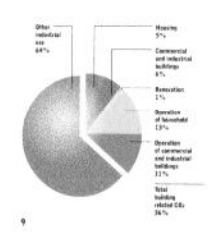

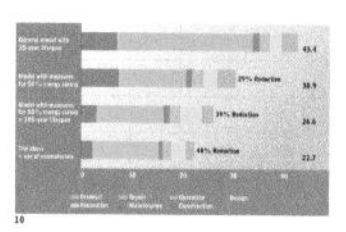

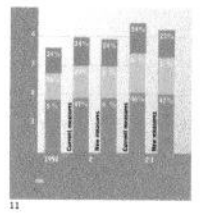

The main method used are deep eaves to keep direct sunlight out of the rooms in summer supplemented by Shitomi (latticed shutters) and Sudare (rattan blinds) (Photos 15, 16, 17). Deciduous trees planted near houses only block sunlight in summer, when they have leaves. Besides using natural energy, these methods lend character and aesthetic features to buildings (photo 18).

Shoji screens for pleasant lighting

Shoji screens are a traditional way of drawing light in and dispersing it throughout a room. The appearance of the screens varies with changing patterns of daylight and shadow, creating a sense of connection between interior and exterior (photos 19, 20).

Uchimizu (sprayed water) to use the transpiration effect

Water sprayed on paths, courtyards and elsewhere makes use of the water's latent heat of evaporation to lower the air temperature (photo 21).

Engawa (wood-floored verandah)

The Engawa or verandah space is interposed as a buffer between the outside and the "zashiki" rooms (living rooms with tatami mat floors). Daylight passing through the shoji screens is dispersed throughout the rooms within. n ne weather the shoji and other barriers can be thrown open to let the breeze from outside flow into the living space, or closed to varying degrees to regulate the flow of hot outside air to the living rooms. The engawa is a space for drawing in and using natural energy, while blocking unwanted light and heat. It is also a place to sit quietly and enjoy the natural environment outside (photo 22).

Flexible use of space

The inner rooms of traditional Japanese houses are separated by shoji screens or fusuma (sliding doors) rather than by fixed walls. This construction allows the available space to be partitioned into smaller rooms or merged into larger spaces as required by the occupants and their activities.

The flexible use of space in Japanese traditional architecture (photos 23 and 2). By removing the shoji screen in summer, we can enjoy an open-air atmosphere. When the shoji screen is in place, we can appreciate the soft sunlight it provides.

The Ireko Concept of Spatial Zoning.

In traditional buildings the elements described in section 3.1 are combined in a spatial composition which enhances their effects and forms a balanced environment that is both comfortable and aesthetically close to nature. Space in Japanese traditional houses is not simply divided between interior and exterior. Instead, a variety of spaces exist in the interstices, creating a pleasantly heterogeneous environment which has real depth while remaining close to nature. The basis of the Ireko concept is the spatial flow from outdoor space through to semi-outdoor space, semi-indoor space, indoor space and local indoor spaces. We aim to take the traditional Ireko concept of space as our model, to redefine it from a new viewpoint, and put that concept into effect in spaces that harness the benefits of nature to minimize the environmental load (figure 12).

Outdoor Spaces

The landscape and greenery outside a traditional building serve to moderate the harsher outside environment and are essential for the formation of a pleasant, self-balancing indoor space. n a broader environmental level, the area of paved ground is reduced, limiting the heat island effect and absorbing rain to replenish groundwater. The foliage preserves privacy by blocking lines of sight, baffles noise and absorbs CO_2. Natural topography and original flora should be retained to avoid standardized uniformity in the landscaping design (photos 25, 26).

Intermediate Spaces

The intermediate spaces that exist between indoors and outdoors are particularly important for defining the relationship between the two. Within the "Ireko" spatial hierarchy they can be divided between the semi-outdoor and the semi-indoor areas.

Rodai (balconies or decks) are the main type of semi-outdoor space. They are not completely outdoors, but they're very close. They have some degree of

Introduction, opening pages.

Technical essays, typical double page.

Contents

Inter
Insti

Location:
Kyoto

Site area:
40,166 m²

Building area:
5,251 m²

1.5 The south façade show
the research facilities in a
traditional Ganko (tier)
arrangement with a reflect
pond. The plan evokes a
quiet and open environmen
1.6 Seminar lounge of the
research block with a view
the garden.

and the surrour

The Architectural Cor
IIAS is situatec
Prefecture that
architectural hi
the seat of the

screens, tatami
Such temple an
many ancient b
to see how the
the architectura
The arri
a lasting impac

Table of contents. The layout is based on the 12x15 unit modular grid.

Microtypography. Grid units determine typesizes and interline space, hanging sub-titles, and paragraph indents.

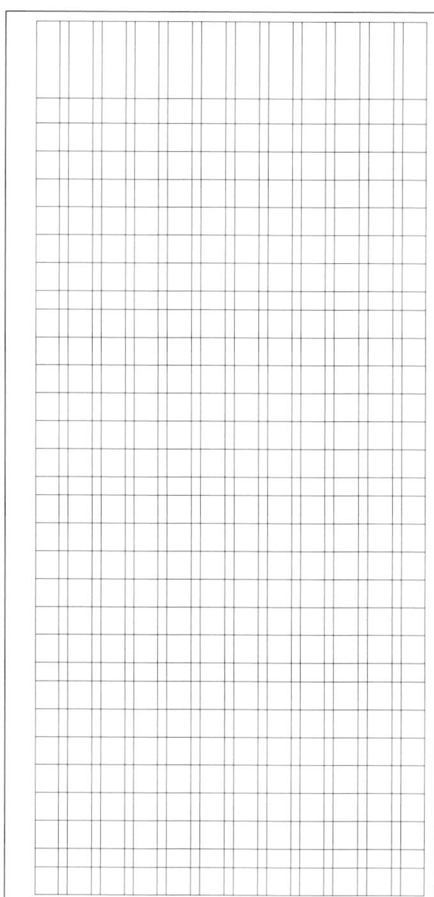

Schematic composition of primary information elements.

Finely detailed grid derived from the design requirements of the information.

Composition of the lecture information with superimposed grid structure.

Monday

Nigel Coates
Achitect, London

Exploring Ecsta-city

Coates

Design of a poster announcing ten lectures, five exhibitions, and one symposium held over a four-month period at Columbia University. The composition originated in the typographic information.

Lectures are arranged in four tiers, according to month. One lecture is shifted to emphasize its open date at the time the poster was printed. The exhibitions are grouped on the top right for prominence and to contrast with the block of lectures. The symposium, a secondary event, is placed towards the end of the schedule.

To differentiate the ten lectures, each is treated as a unique typographic composition. The lectures are placed against a gray background to create a window effect that alludes to a building.

The finely detailed grid structure, accounting for the individual typographic compositions of the lecture data, was developed after the basic composition of information elements was established.

Columbia Architecture Planning Preservation

Lectures

6:30pm
Wood Auditorium
Avery Hall

Doors open to
the general public
6:15pm

Exhibitions

Spring 2001

January 29–March 2
Masters of the Camera: Photography by Bernd and Hilla Becher
400 Avery Hall

March 26–May 4
LA12
100 Avery Hall

February 4–March 9
Space, Color and Clarity: Luis Barragan Photographed by René Burri
100 Avery Hall

April 9–May 4
UTAP/Assisting Urban Regeneration: From the Dwelling Unit to the City Scale
400 Avery Hall

May 12–June 1
End of Year Student Exhibition
Avery and Buell Hall Galleries

January

Monday 22
Coates
Nigel Coates
Architect, London
Exploring Ecsta-city

February

Wednesday 7
Decq
Odile Decq
Architect, Paris
Recent Work

Wednesday 21
LOT/EK
LOT/EK
Ada Tolla +
Giuseppe Lignano
Urban Scan

To be announced
Hadid
Zaha Hadid
Architect, London

March

Wednesday 7
Field Operations
Stan Allen
Associate Professor of Architecture, Columbia University
+
James Corner
Landscape Architect, Chair/Professor of Landscape Architecture University of Pennsylvania
Field Operations

Monday 19
Prix
Wolf Prix
Coop Himmelblau Architects
Vienna, Guadalajara
The Himmelblau Project

Wednesday 28
Douglis
Evan Douglis
Architect, New York
Adjunct Assistant Professor of Architecture
Columbia University
Museum of Accidents

New Urbanisms

A dialogue with Margaret Crawford, Kenneth Frampton, Mark Robbins moderated by David Smiley, co-sponsored by the MS in Architecture and Urban Design Program, Columbia University and the Van Alen Institute.

February 27, 2001
6:00–8:30pm
Van Alen Institute
30 West 22nd Street

April

Monday 2
Cousins
Mark Cousins
Head, Graduate Histories and Theories Program, Architectural Association, London
Visiting Professor of Architecture, Columbia University
The Ugly

Wednesday 11
Spuybroek
Lars Spuybroek
Architect
Rotterdam
Visiting Associate Professor of Architecture, Columbia University
Mold and Matrix

Friday 13
Castells
Manuel Castells
Professor of City and Regional Planning, University of California at Berkeley
Space of Flows, Space of Places
Toward a Theory of Urbanism in the Information Age

Buell Evening Lecture sponsored by Skidmore, Owings, and Merrill

Final poster
12x24 in.

Columbia University Graduate School of Architecture, Planning and Preservation. Lectures and Exhibitions Fall 1985. Wednesday Lecture Series. 6:00 PM, Wood Auditorium, Avery Hall. Exhibitions, 100 Level, Avery Hall. **1**

October 2. Werner Seligman, Architect, Dean, School of Architecture, Syracuse University; Frank Lloyd Wright: The Evolution of the Prairie House. **2**

October 9. Sam Bass Warner, Jr., William Edwards Huntington Professor of History, Boston University; The Awful History and Fresh Promise of Urban Gardens. **3**

October 16. Jonathan Barnett, Urban Designer, New York, NY; The Elusive City: Five Centuries of Design, Ambition and Miscalculation. **4**

October 23. Melvin Charney, Architect and Artist, Montreal; Constructs and Construction. **5**

October 30. John Jacobus, Professor of Art History, Dartmouth College; The Haunted House of Modern Architecture. **6**

November 6. Max Bond, Dean, School of Architecture and Environmental Studies, City College of the City University of New York; My Work. **7**

November 13. William Pedersen, Architect, Kohn Pedersen Fox, New York, NY; Recent Work. **8**

November 20. Rafael Moneo, Architect, Chairman, Graduate School of Design, Harvard University; To be announced. **9**

December 4. Diana Balmori, Partner, Cesar Pelli & Associates, New Haven, CT; Campus: Rural, Suburban, Urban; Notes for a New Synthesis. **10**

September 23–October 18. Tianjin University, China; Student Work. **11**

October 21–November 15. Three Firms: Steven Holl Architects, New York, NY; UKZ, Ithaca, NY; Giuseppe Zambonini, New York, NY **12**

November 18–December 6. Fred Thompson University of Waterloo, Waterloo, Ontario, Canada; Ritual Renewal of Space in Kakunodate and Shiraiwa. **13**

Typographic information separated into 13 parts: the school's name; lecture time and location; nine lectures; and three exhibitions.

Design of a poster announcing a series of lectures and exhibitions held over a three-month period at Columbia University Graduate School of Architecture, Planning and Preservation. The composition originated in the typographic information.

The poster's format, based on two squares, initiated the concept of working with the typographic information as square units. When treated as squares, the typographic information can be easily grouped and moved around to explore various visual compositions.

The 5:3:1 ratio of lectures per month determined the stepped composition of nine squares. The composition of type and graphic elements adheres to the square units.

The exhibition information was converted into narrow vertical rectangles for contrast.

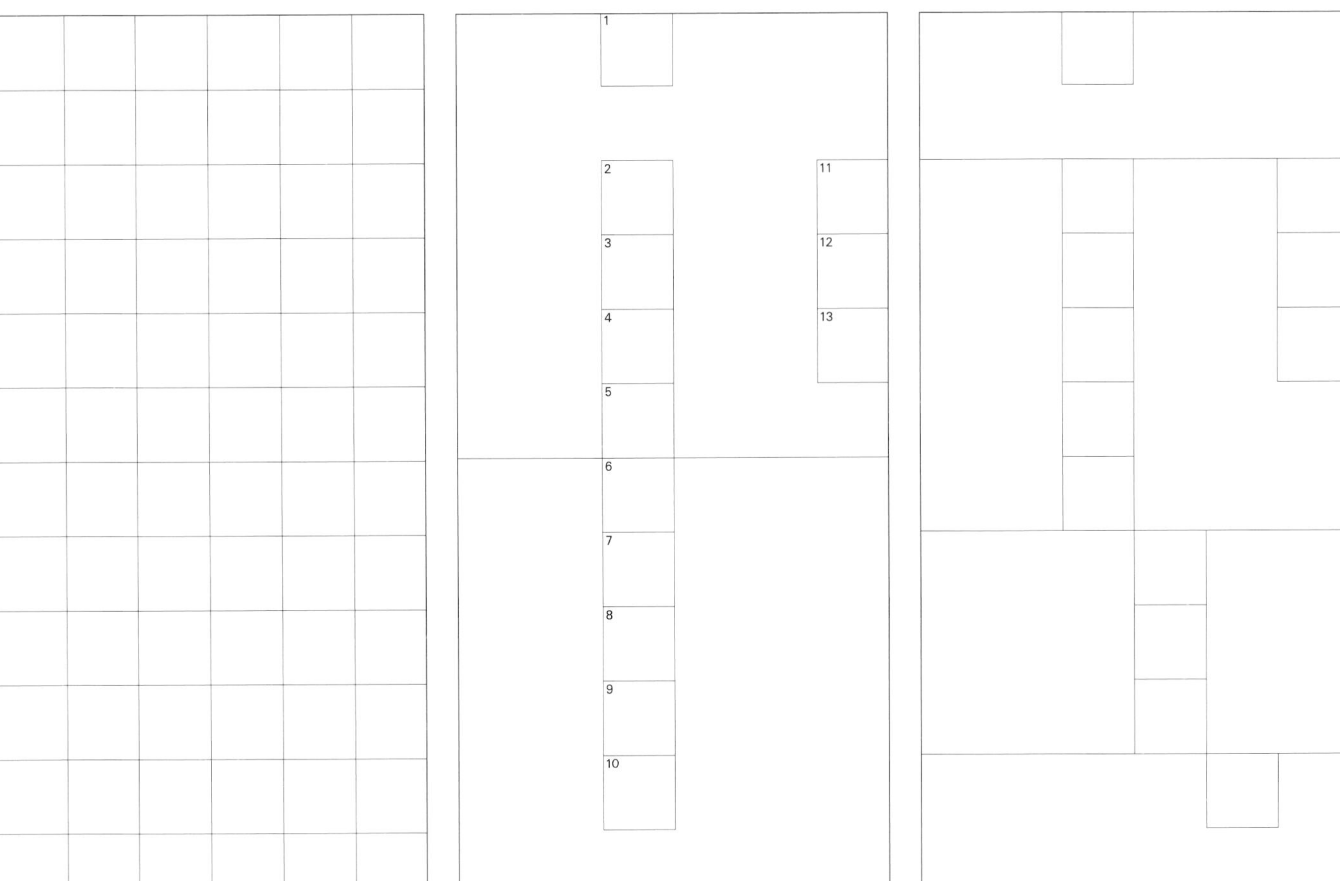

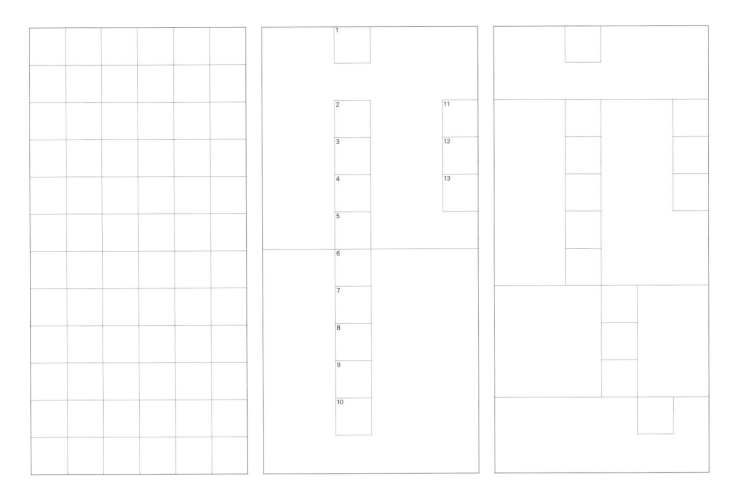

Double square format subdivided into 6x12 square units.

Preliminary empirical composition of 13 typographic parts.

Intermediate, visually more active composition of 13 typographic parts.

Werner Seligman
Architect, Dean
School of Architecture
Syracuse University
Frank Lloyd Wright:
The Evolution
of the Prairie House

Lectures
and
Exhibitions

Wednesday
Lecture
Series

The composition of the line and dot pattern derives from the square unit.

Microtypography.
The three type sizes and interline space are based on 15, 11, and 7 lines per square unit.

Columbia University
Graduate School
of Architecture, Planning
and Preservation

Lectures
and
Exhibitions
Fall 1985

Wednesday
Lecture
Series

6:00 PM
Wood Auditorium
Avery Hall

Oct :

2 *Werner Seligman*
Architect, Dean
School of Architecture
Syracuse University
'Frank Lloyd Wright:
The Evolution
of the Prairie House'

9 *Sam Bass Warner, Jr.*
William Edwards Huntington
Professor of History
Boston University
'The Awful History and
Fresh Promise
of Urban Gardens'

16 *Jonathan Barnett*
Urban Designer
New York, NY
'The Elusive City:
Five Centuries of Design,
Ambition and
Miscalculation'

23 *Melvin Charney*
Architect and Artist
Montréal, Canada
'Constructs
and Construction'

30 *John Jacobus*
Professor of Art History
Dartmouth College
'The Haunted House
of Modern Architecture'

Nov :

6 *Max Bond*
Dean, School of Architecture
and Environmental Studies
City College of the
City University of New York
'My Work'

13 *William Pedersen*
Architect
Kohn Pedersen Fox
New York, NY
'Recent Work'

20 *Rafael Moneo*
Architect, Chairman
Graduate School of Design
Harvard University
'To be announced'

Dec :

4 *Diana Balmori*
Partner
Cesar Pelli & Associates
New Haven, CT
'Campus: Rural, Suburban,
Urban: Notes for a New
Synthesis'

100 Level
Avery Hall

Exhibitions

SEP 23-
OCT 18
Tianjin University
China
'Student Work'

OCT 21-
NOV 15
Three Firms

Steven Holl
Architects
New York, NY

UKZ
Ithaca, NY

Giuseppe
Zambonini
New York, NY

NOV 18-
DEC 6
Fred Thompson
University
of Waterloo
Waterloo, Ontario
Canada

'Ritual Renewal
of Space
in Kakunodate
and Shiraiwa'

Design: Willi Kunz Associates, New York

Final poster
12 x 24 in.

Fredrich Cantor Photographs
March 2–30
Robert Schoelkopf Gallery
825 Madison Avenue, New York

Raw typographic information.

Typographic information divided according to syntax structure.

Photograph with vertical subdivisions.

Fredrich Cantor	**1**
Photographs	**2**
March 2–30	**3**
Robert Schoelkopf Gallery	**4**
825 Madison Avenue New York	**5**

Design of a poster announcing an exhibition of photographs of New York City by Fredrich Cantor. The composition was inspired by a photograph.

The poster image was chosen for its powerful structure, clear proportions, and strong contrast. The image structure determined the vertical subdivisions of the poster format and the major alignments of the typography. The strong contrast of the image extends to the typographic composition characterized by bold/light, open/closed, large/small, and the straight/angular contrast of the black borders.

The photograph's height is one third of the poster's vertical dimension. The horizontal subdivisions at the bottom derive from dividing one third of the poster into eight units.

The typographic information consists of five parts: artist's name, exhibition title, date, location, and address.

The spacing of the exhibition date relates to the building's windows.

Primary vertical alignments subdividing the space.

Horizontal alignment lines derive from dividing the bottom third of the space into eight units.

Fredrich **Cantor**

M A R C H

2 - 3 0

Photographs

Robert Schoelkopf Gallery

825 Madison Avenue
New York

Typographic information with superimposed alignment lines.

F r e d r i c h **Cantor**

M A R C H

2 - 3 0

Photographs

Robert Schoelkopf Gallery 825 Madison Avenue New York

Final poster
16x22 in.

The Future of the Past, Keene Valley Keene

Adirondack Center Museum. Elizabethtown, New York

August 18–September 20
Opening, August 18, 5:00–7:00 pm

Architectural Projects by Students at the Columbia University Graduate School of Architecture, Planning and Preservation. Richard Plunz, critic

Photographs by Nathan Farb

Sponsored in part by the New York State Council of the Arts

Toby Chaum, Enid de Gracia, Javier de la Garza, Jessica Drury, Doris Kim, Ned Lager, John la Vecchia, Kimberly Miller, Dan Nation, Ethan Nelson, Mary Patera, Cordelia Pitman, Arthur Platt, Michael Poloukhine, Joel Towers, Adam van Doran, Michael White, Gene Young

The Future of the Past **1**
Keene Valley Keene

Adirondack Center Museum **2**
Elizabethtown, New York

August 18–September 20 **3**

Opening **4**
August 18, 5:00–7:00 pm

Architectural Projects by Students at the **5**
Columbia University
Graduate School of Architecture, Planning and Preservation
Richard Plunz, critic

Photographs by Nathan Farb **6**

Sponsored in part by the New York State Council of the Arts **7**

Toby Chaum **8**
Enid de Gracia
Javier de la Garza
Jessica Drury
Doris Kim
Ned Lager
John la Vecchia
Kimberly Miller
Dan Nation
Ethan Nelson
Mary Patera
Cordelia Pitman
Arthur Platt
Michael Poloukhine
Joel Towers
Adam van Doran
Michael White
Gene Young

Typographic information with minimal syntax structure.

Typographic information in two parts with differentiated syntax structure.

Design of a poster announcing an exhibition of urban design projects from a summer course held in mountainous upstate New York. The typographic information consists of two major parts: one, the exhibit title, location, opening and closing date, and the time and date of the opening reception; and two, the names of the critic, photographer, sponsors, and students.

The composition of part one, connoting mountains, space, and time, is created using a visual structure derived from an imaginary sketch of Keene Valley. The composition of part two is created using a predetermined grid structure, which evolved by dividing the format into ten columns of 10.5 picas. The 10.5 pica measure was also applied in creating the 7 rows. The 10.5 pica units are subdivided into seven lines of 16 point type with 18 point interline space.

1

2

3

4

5

6

7

8

Schematic distribution of the eight typographic information components.

An imaginary sketch serves as the basis for the visual composition of the first four components.

A predetermined structure serves as the basis for the composition of the remaining four components. The short lines of student names determine the narrow columns.

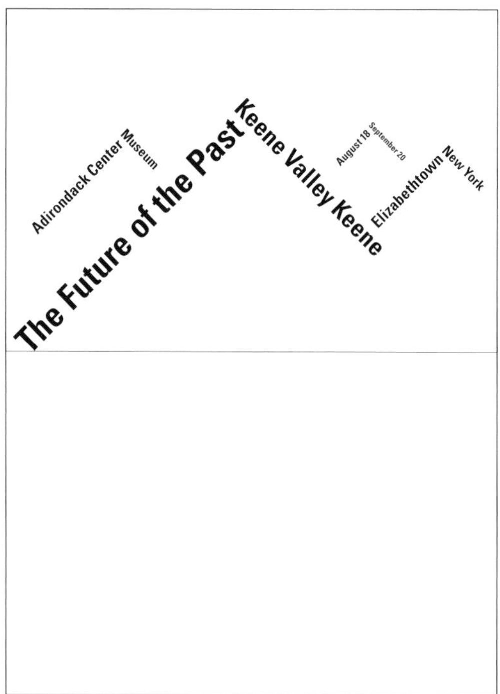

Ethan Nelson
Mary Patera
Cordelia Pitman
Arthur Platt

Ned Lager
John la Vecchia
Kimberly Miller
Dan Nation

Toby Chaum
Enid de Gracia
Javier de la Garza
Jessica Drury
Doris Kim

The typographic information in components one through four is transformed into the visual structure using different type sizes and orientations.

Typographic components five through eight are composed according to the grid structure. Each column measures 10.5 picas, which also corresponds to the typographic measurements of 16 point Univers 67 with 18 point interline space (7 lines = 10.5 picas).

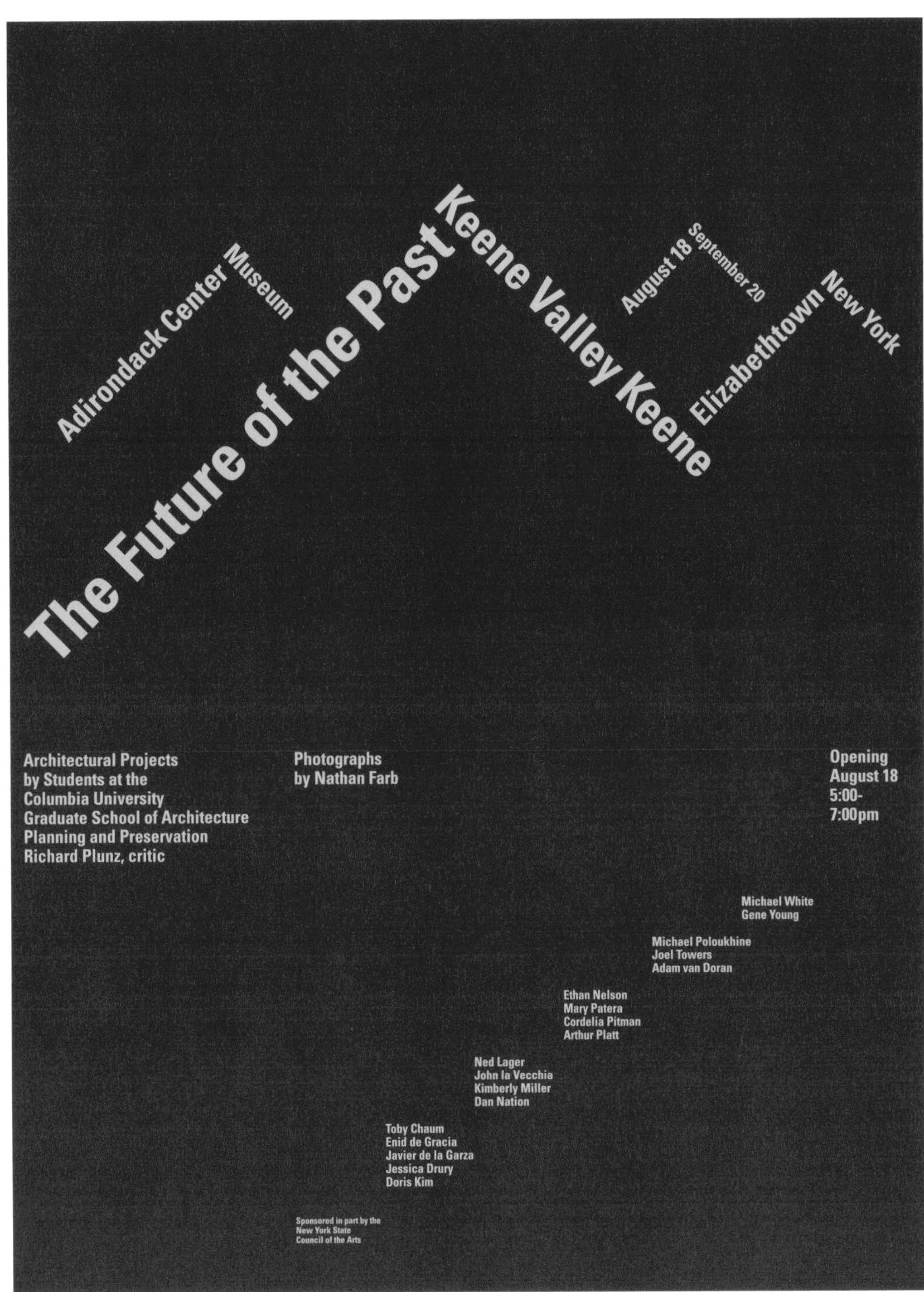

Final poster
18 x 24 in.

Graduate Program 1

The Ohio State University. The Department of Industrial Design offers a graduate program of study in Design to students with diverse educational and professional experience, leading to the Master of Arts degree.

The practice of Design has become increasingly broad in scope and complex in application. Contemporary design requires a comprehensive knowledge of social, psychological, cultural, technological, institutional and political forces that shape the man-made environment and influence natural environments. Facing the challenge of this complexity, it is the responsibility of the designer to guide the evolution of balanced physical and organizational conditions satisfying expected human needs. To enhance the vital elements of human interaction with the designed environment, a positive, value-directed philosophy of action is encouraged. Integrative, flexible approaches to generalized problem-solving are emphasized. An atmosphere of innovation and open experimentation is maintained.

The program has been structured to be responsive to current and anticipated requirements of professional practice in visual communication, product and space-enclosure design. An assessment of these requirements has led to the recognition of four distinct specializations:

Design Planning and Analysis 2

Planning of the design process, with emphasis on the utilization of appropriate methods of analysis and synthesis.

Design Development 3

Conceptualization and realization of visual communication, product and space-enclosure systems, emphasizing preparation for production.

Design Administration 4

Organization and management of design activity in governmental, consultive, corporate and advocatory situations.

Design Education 5

Development, instruction and evaluation of design-related knowledge and skills at the university or equivalent level.

In addition to the selection of one of these specializations, students enrolled in the program are encouraged to maintain and develop an existing or complementary professional or academic expertise. With a faculty assembled from a variety of academic and professional backgrounds, an open learning environment has been established which takes advantage of the diverse facilities and expertise available at the university.

After completing the program, the graduate is in a unique position to continue a career while participating in the development of innovative approaches to dealing with the complexity of the contemporary human environment.

Financial Assistance. A limited number of paid teaching and research associateships (including tuition fee waiver) are available.

For further information, write to:
Graduate Committee Chairman
The Ohio State University
Department of Industrial Design
128 North Oval Drive,
Columbus, Ohio 43210
Telephone 614 422 6746

Typographic information with the five key components.

Design of a poster announcing a graduate program in design at the Ohio State University. The composition originated in the typographic information consisting of five parts: an introduction to the program and four short descriptions of the areas of specialization.

Developing a precise relationship between the five titles was key to the typographic solution. Various compositions were explored to visually link the poster title and the longest of the specialization titles.

The eight columns derive from the difference in length of the two titles. The word design is set bold to match the width of two columns. Each of the eight columns is subdivided into five units. All vertical alignments correspond with these subunits. The line space between Design and Planning and Analysis determines the fourteen horizontal subdivisions.

Although the final solution appears deceptively simple, this process of transforming typographic information is still demanding for the inexperienced designer.

Graduate Program

Design Planning and Analysis

Graduate Program

Design
Planning and Analysis

Graduate Program

Design
Planning and Analysis

Graduate Program

Design Planning and Analysis

Graduate Program

Design
Planning and Analysis

Graduate Program

Design
Planning and Analysis

Graduate Program

Design Planning and Analysis

Graduate Program

Design
Planning and Analysis

Graduate Program

Design
Planning and Analysis

Columns one and two. Exploration of different compositions with information components one and two.

Column three Development of final structure. The optically matching bold underline reinforces the word design.

Graduate Program

The Ohio State University
The Department of Industrial Design offers a graduate program of study in Design to students with diverse educational and professional experience, leading to the Master of Arts degree.

The practice of Design has become increasingly broad in scope and complex in application. Contemporary design requires a comprehensive knowledge of social, psychological, cultural, technological, institutional and political forces that shape the man-made environment and influence natural environments. Facing the challenge of this complexity, it is the responsibility of the designer to guide the evolution of balanced physical and organizational conditions satisfying expected human needs. To enhance the vital elements of human interaction with the designed environment, a positive, value-directed philosophy of action is encouraged. Integrative, flexible approaches to generalized problem-solving are emphasized. An atmosphere of innovation and open experimentation is maintained.

The program has been structured to be responsive to current and anticipated requirements of professional practice in visual communication, product and space-enclosure design. An assessment of these requirements has led to the recognition of four distinct specializations:

Design

Planning and Analysis

Planning of the design process, with emphasis on the utilization of appropriate methods of analysis and synthesis.

Design

Development

Conceptualization and realization of visual communication, product and space-enclosure systems, emphasizing preparation for production.

Design

Administration

Organization and management of design activity in governmental, consultive, corporate and advocatory situations.

Design

Education

Development, instruction and evaluation of design-related knowledge and skills at the university or equivalent level.

In addition to the selection of one of these specializations, students enrolled in the program are encouraged to maintain and develop an existing or complementary professional or academic expertise. With a faculty assembled from a variety of academic and professional backgrounds, an open learning environment has been established which takes advantage of the diverse facilities and expertise available at the university.

After completing the program, the graduate is in a unique position to continue a career while participating in the development of innovative approaches to dealing with the complexity of the contemporary human environment.

Financial Assistance
A limited number of paid teaching and research associateships (including tuition fee waiver) are available.

For further information, write to:
Graduate Committee Chairman
The Ohio State University
Department of Industrial Design
128 North Oval Drive
Columbus, Ohio 43210

Telephone: 614 422 6746

Information with superimposed structure. The subunits indicated at the bottom determine the alignment, indent, and width of the texts.

Graduate Program

The Ohio State University
The Department of Industrial Design offers a graduate program of study in Design to students with diverse educational and professional experience, leading to the Master of Arts degree.

The practice of Design has become increasingly broad in scope and complex in application. Contemporary design requires a comprehensive knowledge of social, psychological, cultural, technological, institutional and political forces that shape the man-made environment and influence natural environments. Facing the challenge of this complexity, it is the responsibility of the designer to guide the evolution of balanced physical and organizational conditions satisfying expected human needs. To enhance the vital elements of human interaction with the designed environment, a positive, value-directed philosophy of action is encouraged. Integrative, flexible approaches to generalized problem-solving are emphasized. An atmosphere of innovation and open experimentation is maintained.

The program has been structured to be responsive to current and anticipated requirements of professional practice in visual communication, product and space-enclosure design. An assessment of these requirements has led to the recognition of four distinct specializations:

Design
Planning and Analysis

Planning of the design process, with emphasis on the utilization of appropriate methods of analysis and synthesis.

Design
Development

Conceptualization and realization of visual communication, product and space-enclosure systems, emphasizing preparation for production.

Design
Administration

Organization and management of design activity in governmental, consultive, corporate and advocatory situations.

Design
Education

Development, instruction and evaluation of design-related knowledge and skills at the university or equivalent level.

In addition to the selection of one of these specializations, students enrolled in the program are encouraged to maintain and develop an existing or complementary professional or academic expertise. With a faculty assembled from a variety of academic and professional backgrounds, an open learning environment has been established which takes advantage of the diverse facilities and expertise available at the university.

After completing the program, the graduate is in a unique position to continue a career while participating in the development of innovative approaches to dealing with the complexity of the contemporary human environment.

Financial Assistance
A limited number of paid teaching and research associateships (including tuition fee waiver) are available.

For further information, write to:
Graduate Committee Chairman
The Ohio State University
Department of Industrial Design
128 North Oval Drive
Columbus, Ohio 43210

Telephone: 614 422 6746

Final Poster
18x24 in.

3

Topology of typography

At the core of typographic design is a set of information and a context. From these conditions the designer develops a conceptual idea.

As the concept evolves into a design, the topology emerges from the form and relationships of the typographic elements. The topology is then captured in a series of diagrams that delineate the surface structure of the design.

The process allows evaluation of the design in multiple layers, while also giving the designer a tool for refining, altering, adjusting, deconstructing and reassembling the individual layers to create a cohesive typographic solution.

The topology of typography conveys the visual depth of a design and provides inspiration for creating new contours on known ground.

The character of a place or an object is partially expressed by its surface topology.

The topology of a fabric derives from weaving two linear elements, the warp and the woof, at a ninety-degree angle. Cutting and assembling the cloth according to a sewing pattern creates the topology of a dress. A landscape's topology comes from its physical features such as mountains, valleys, rivers, and forests.

Typography, too, has a topology. The surface characteristics of typography are the optical elevations created by the arrangement of typographic elements: the large components rise to the foreground, the small elements recede into the background. On a text page, the paragraph indents and the short lines ending the paragraphs create the desired optical elevation. A page without elevations is monotonous and dull.

The topology of a landscape is abstracted in the construction of a map, just as architectural drawings and building materials define the topology of a building. Typography has its own innate topology that can be summarized in a series of diagrams tracing the position of typographic elements. As with other kinds of maps, the diagram helps the designer to move between working with abstract relationships and working with the concrete details of the design.

Typographic design begins with a set of information and a context, which the designer uses to generate the conceptual idea. As the concept evolves into a design, the topology emerges and is captured as a series of diagrams delineating the shapes and relationships of the typographic elements. The diagram is not developed a priori for formal purposes. It is based on the information or responds to diagrams established earlier in the process.

In the early stages of design, a topology diagram is used as guide for positioning typographic information. The diagram helps structure multiple layers of information, and aids positioning of typographic elements in precise relationship to one another. I consider the diagram as a test for the conceptual idea. It serves as the intermediary between the sketch and the comprehensive layout. Unlike the static, permanent grid structure, the diagrammatic configuration is open to change.

Based on the first step, a diagram of the secondary level of information is developed, and the way typographic elements intersect in a design is precisely worked out. As a result, the intersecting elements create new micro-aesthetic details that otherwise would not occur. When based on a predetermined grid structure, the typographic elements function side by side with little interaction between them, as if moving on separate tracks. Working diagrammatically encourages breaking this mold. Information elements are arranged in intersecting layers that are flexible, versatile, and can be shifted to implement the conceptual idea.

The diagram is both generative and descriptive. As a generative device the typographic diagram initiates a series of steps, each one building on the previous action to realize the conceptual idea. The diagram can also serve as a mnemonic device, or as a catalyst for the design's aesthetic enhancement and additional conceptual ideas. As a descriptive device, the typographic diagram traces the design development from the conceptual idea to the finished design. It is a record of the evolution of the design process.

Diagrammatic thinking and working is a highly creative approach to realizing a conceptual idea. As a creative device, the diagram leads to new typographic directions. The diagram is not a final design, but an intermediary, a means to an end and a source of inspiration. In approaching typography as a series of adjustable diagrams rather than rigidly structured information, new possibilities for form and communication emerge.

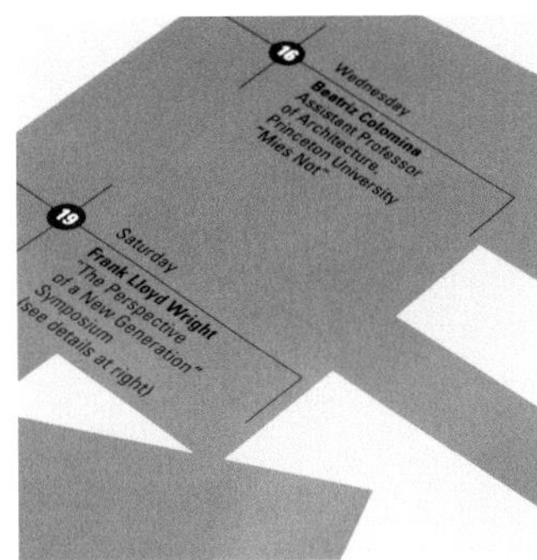

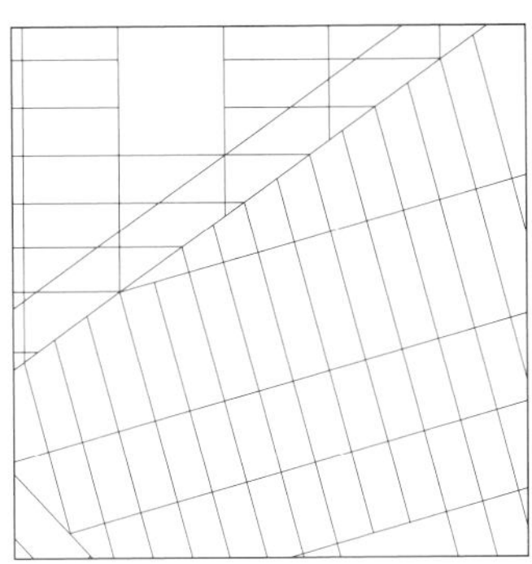

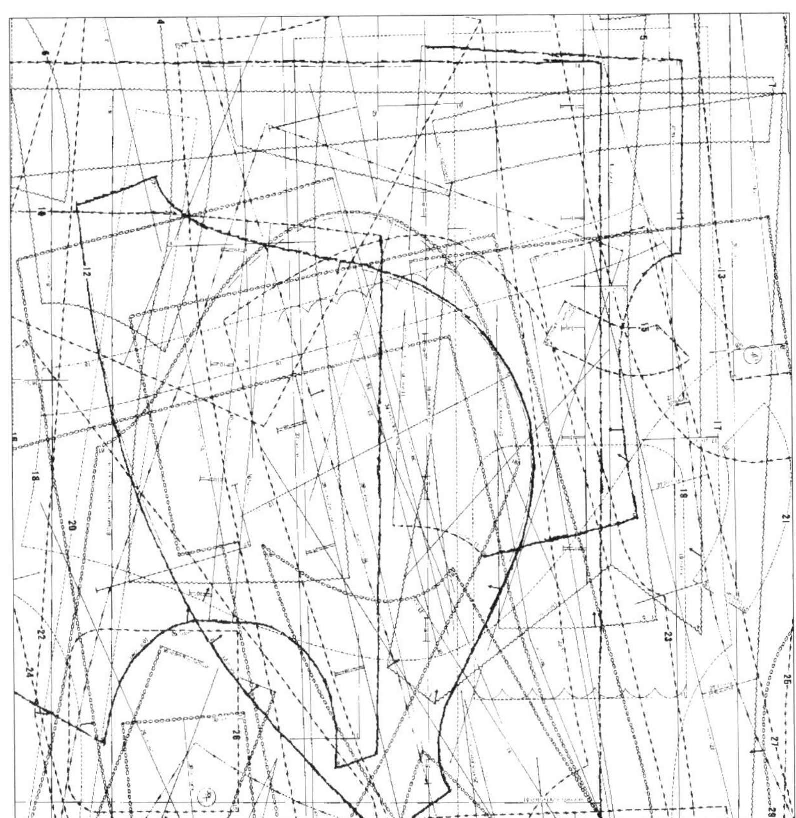

Column one
Topology of a multi-level freeway as a metaphor for typographic information. The reader accesses information at the macro- and microaesthetic level, from different directions, and at different speeds.

Topology of typography.

The sewing pattern defines the topology of a dress.

Column two
Topology of an urban area with minimal optical elevation.

Topology diagram of urban area.

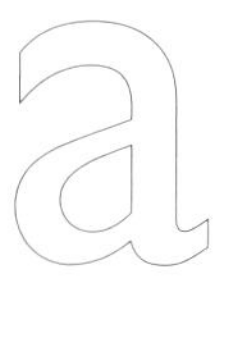

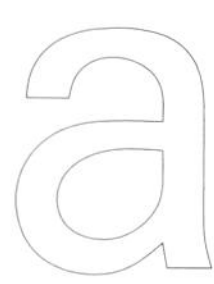

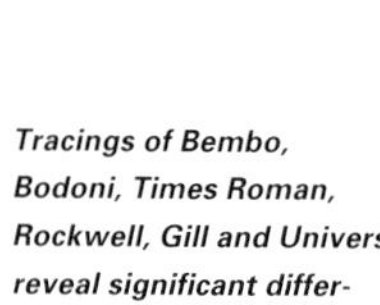

Tracings of Bembo, Bodoni, Times Roman, Rockwell, Gill and Univers reveal significant differences in their topology.

Combined tracings of Bembo, Bodoni, Times Roman, Rockwell, Gill and Univers.

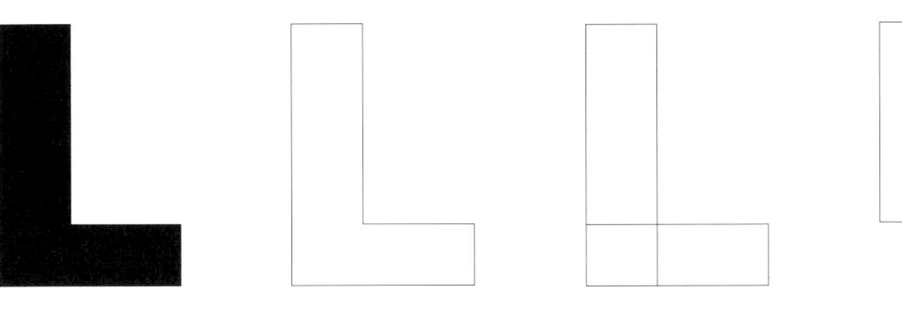

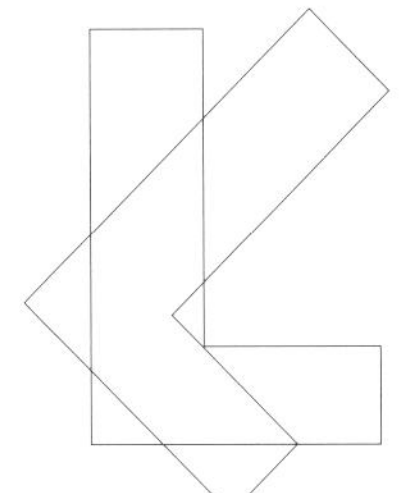

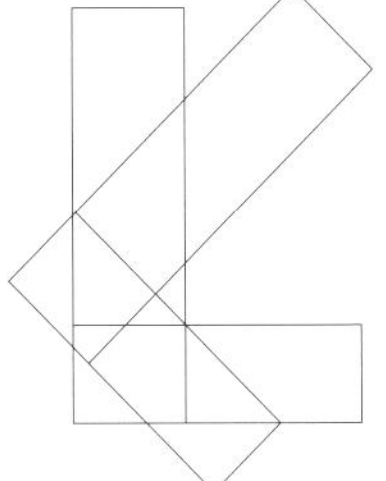

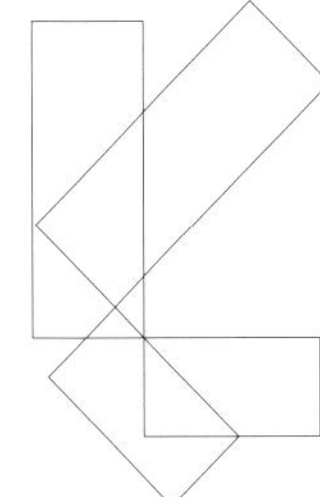

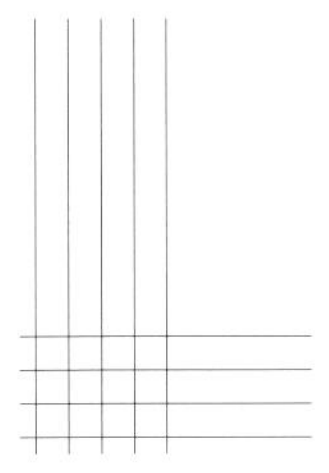

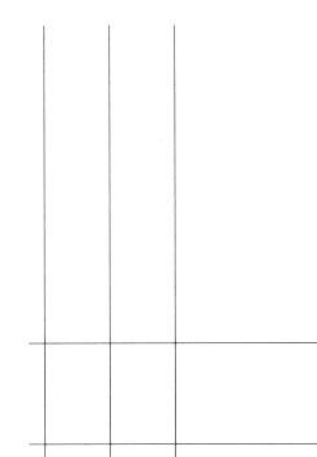

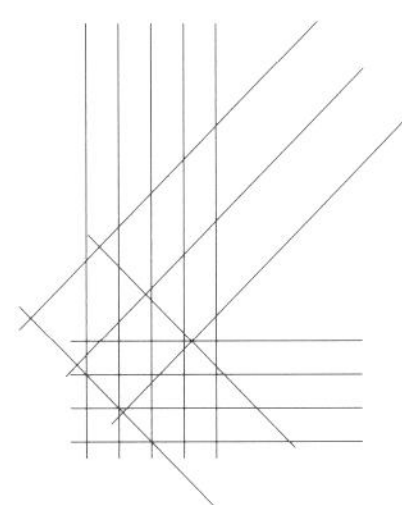

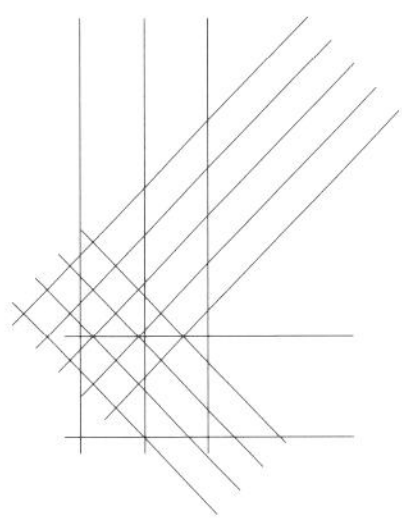

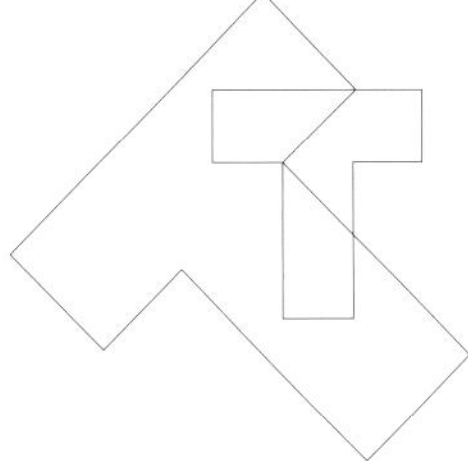

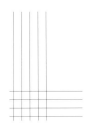

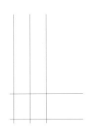

An L form, solid, outlined, as three rectangles, and as two rectangles with an imaginary rectangle completing the form. In each, the topology is more demanding on the viewer.

A second L rotated 45 degrees increases the topology's complexity and makes it cognitively more demanding.

Two L forms composed of different line patterns. The two superimposed L forms oscillate between foreground and back-ground.

Composition of Ts. The size and relative position of the two Ts were determined in diagram-matic form. Visual refinements were made in positive form.

effects are due either to the accretions of time or to its ravages. The city was built at one stroke by Akbar the Magnificent around 1570 and was deserted, but not destroyed, some twenty years later. Though many of the buildings themselves are very fine, the supreme quality of the Mahal-i-Khas lies in its superb proportioning of space. Most of the buildings within and around it are themselves symmetrical in their design, but their spatial setting is never axial. While it is clear at first glance that this is an ordered composition, one looks in vain for the key to it in terms of Western academic art.

It is very difficult for us to get away from the rules of the accepted vision of our Western culture and to realize, even intellectually, that this is not the only way of looking at things. For instance, our eyes in the West have for five hundred years been conditioned, even governed, by another intellectual approach: the single viewpoint. This, though no more intellectual than the acceptance of the dominance of the vertical, is more readily grasped as an acquired characteristic of our vision. It is, however, peculiar to the Western world, where it followed the development of the science of optics: the study of the eye as an inanimate piece of mechanism pinned down upon the board of the scientist.

The optical result was the development of linear perspective: the single vanishing point and the penetration of landscape by a single piercing eye – my eye, my dominating eye. This created a revolution in our way of perceiving the objects around us and in the rational organization of landscape – whether rural or urban. The "view" came into being: the penetration of infinity by means of a guided line – usually an avenue of trees or a symmetrical street. With this came the "vista", the termination of the organized view by an object of interest, often the elaborately symmetrical façade of a large building, that could only be rightly beheld from a central point at some distance from it. All other views were, consciously and unconsciously, accepted as wrong: "This is the place to see it from."

For many it is extremely difficult, even uncomfortable, to accept linear perspective as a conditioned form of vision, limited and partial in its scope. "That is exactly the way it looks to me" is the usual description of a good photograph, for the camera with its single fixed eye expresses linear perspective perfectly. But the rest of the world sees things quite differently.

A Chinese painting is always presented to a spectator whose eye roves along a scroll or up a vertical painting. For instance, in a typical vertical painting of mountain scenery, the spectator will first find himself looking slightly down upon a cottage or fisherman at the foot of the picture, his eye perhaps on the level with the branches of a nearby pine tree. Then he will notice the ascending mountain path, but by now his eye will have moved, and he will be scanning the scenery from a higher vantage point. After a bit his moving eye will light upon a high mountain meadow, or other resting place, and from there, from that viewpoint, he will look up to the inaccessible peaks, half hidden in cloud.

The spectator does not see an instantaneous picture of the entire mountain scene through the peephole of an imaginary camera in the cockpit of a helicopter hovering in mid-air; he participates, through this moving eye, in

76

JICA Hokkaido International Centre

Building a Center for International Understanding

Location:
Obihiro City, Hokkaido

Site area:
4,391 m²

Building area:
2,132 m²

Total floor area:
4,400 m²

Building purpose:
Training facility

Number of floors:
+3, -1

Structure:
RC

Completed:
1996

Residence wing and balconies viewed from the courtyard.

Building a Centre for International Understanding

Hokkaido is the second largest and most northern of the four main islands of Japan. Climatically and geographically, it's an area of contradictions. Local weather patterns are influenced by the marine triangle of the Seas of Okhotsk, Japan and the Pacific, creating many months of harsh winter offset by cool, comfortable summers. The region is home to several rare bio-environments and unique wilderness sites, from the Jozankei Gorge to the Kushiro Swamps. Daisetsu National Park and its mountains comprise the backbone of the island. Sun and rich soils make the area a prominent dairy and crop-farming center, with farms run on an extensive scale.

Located at a latitude of 43 degrees north, the city of Obihiro is renowned for the beauty of its scenery. During winter, cold air masses move down from Siberia and the temperatures drop to minus 20 degrees centigrade below zero while summer temperatures can reach over 30 degrees centigrade.

Obihiro is the location of the Japan International Cooperation Agency, (JICA) that implements the programs of the Official Development Assistance office (ODA). JICA/Hokkaido International Centre is the 11th such ODA center and is founded on "human development, national development and unity among people" The Centre's major focus is 'technology and knowledge

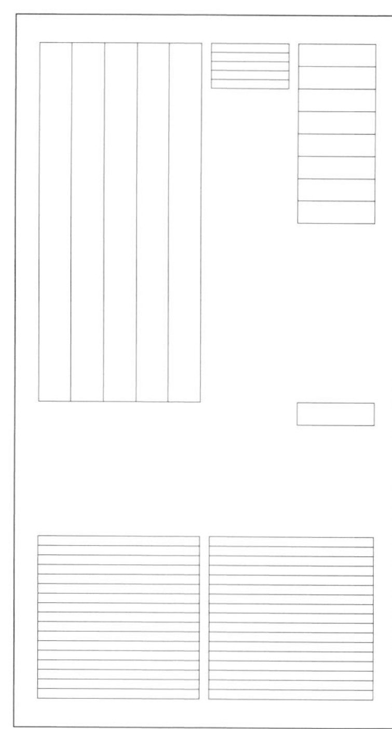

The topology of this text page is created by paragraph indents and short lines ending the paragraphs.

The topology of this project introduction is created by three different typographic textures: vertical title, technical data, and text.

Bernard Tschumi, Dean
Columbia University
Graduate School of Architecture,
Planning and Preservation

requests the pleasure of
your company for the
opening of the exhibition

Morningside Heights: Studio Projects for the Centennial

Tuesday, October 7
5:00–7:00 pm
Reception and viewing

Arthur Ross
Architecture Gallery
Buell Hall
Columbia University

October 7–November 15
Gallery hours:
Tuesday–Saturday 12–6

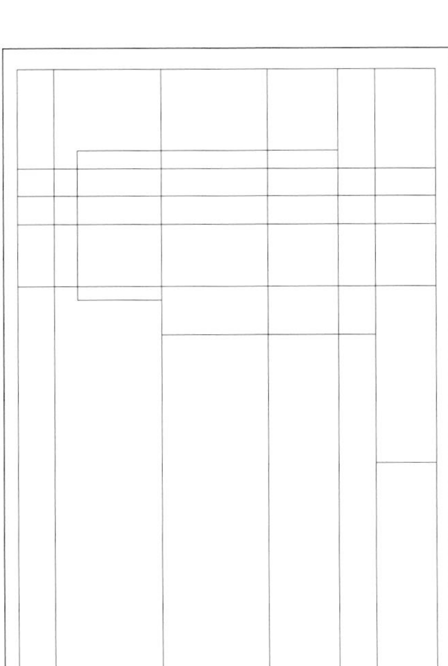

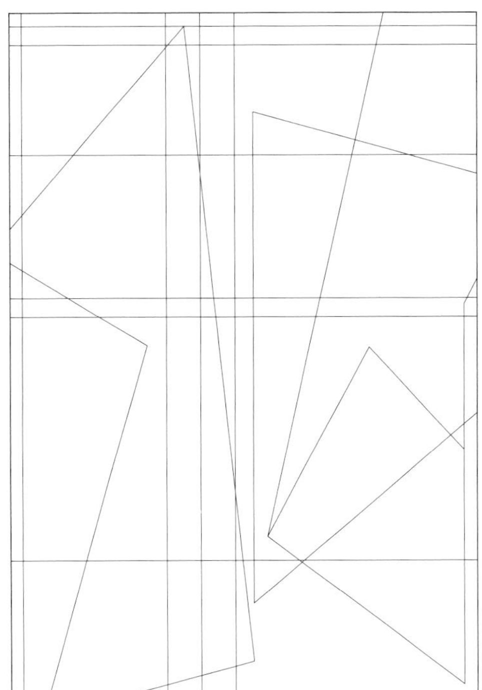

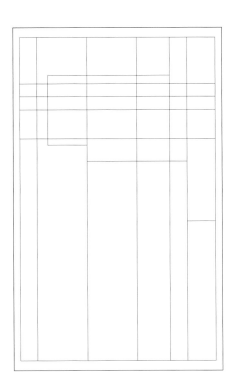

The topology of this invitation is created by the typography in the fore-ground and the gray field in the background.

The topology of this invitation is created by the typography in the foreground and the three-tier background.

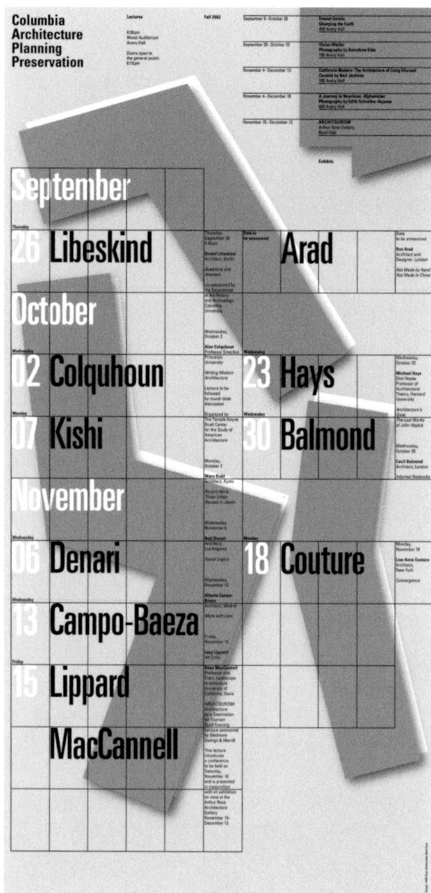

Columbia
Architecture
Planning
Preservation
September
26 Libeskind
Arad
October
02 Colquhoun
23 Hays
07 Kishi
30 Balmond
November
06 Denari
18 Couture
13 Campo-Baeza
15 Lippard
MacCannell

Lecture series poster. The topology comprises five layers, or optical levels.

Level one, the three graphic shapes, alludes to the lecture's architectural themes. The three shapes refer to the three months.

Level two, the grey background with white graphic shapes.

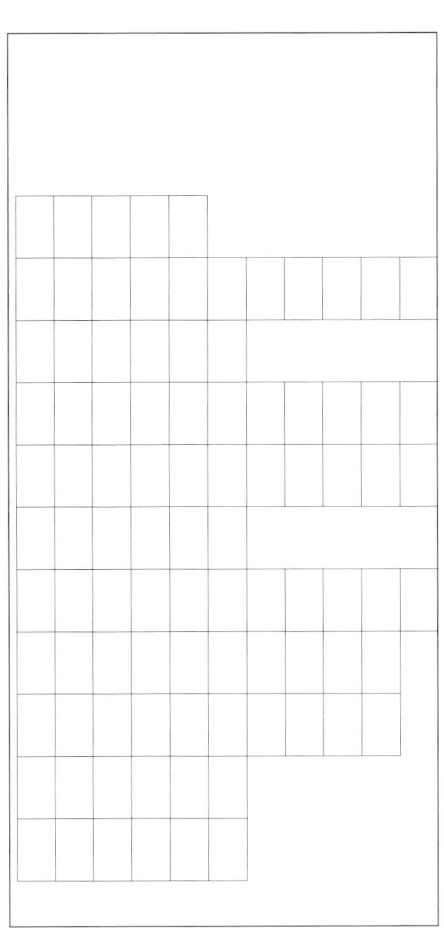

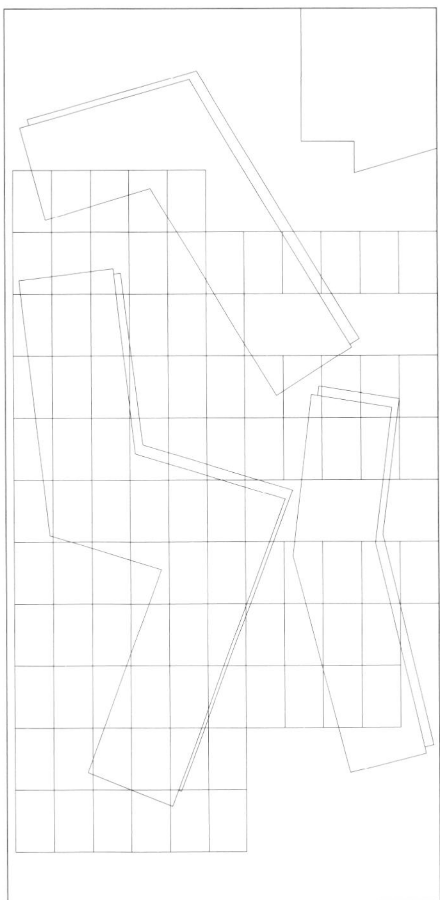

Top row
Level three, typography on the macroaesthetic level, with intermediary grid.

Level four, typography on the microaesthetic level, with intermediary grid.

Level five, the coordinating structure functioning as an intermediary between levels three and four.

Bottom
Diagram of levels one and two combined with intermediary grid. Contrast between orthogonal grid and visual composition of the graphic shapes.

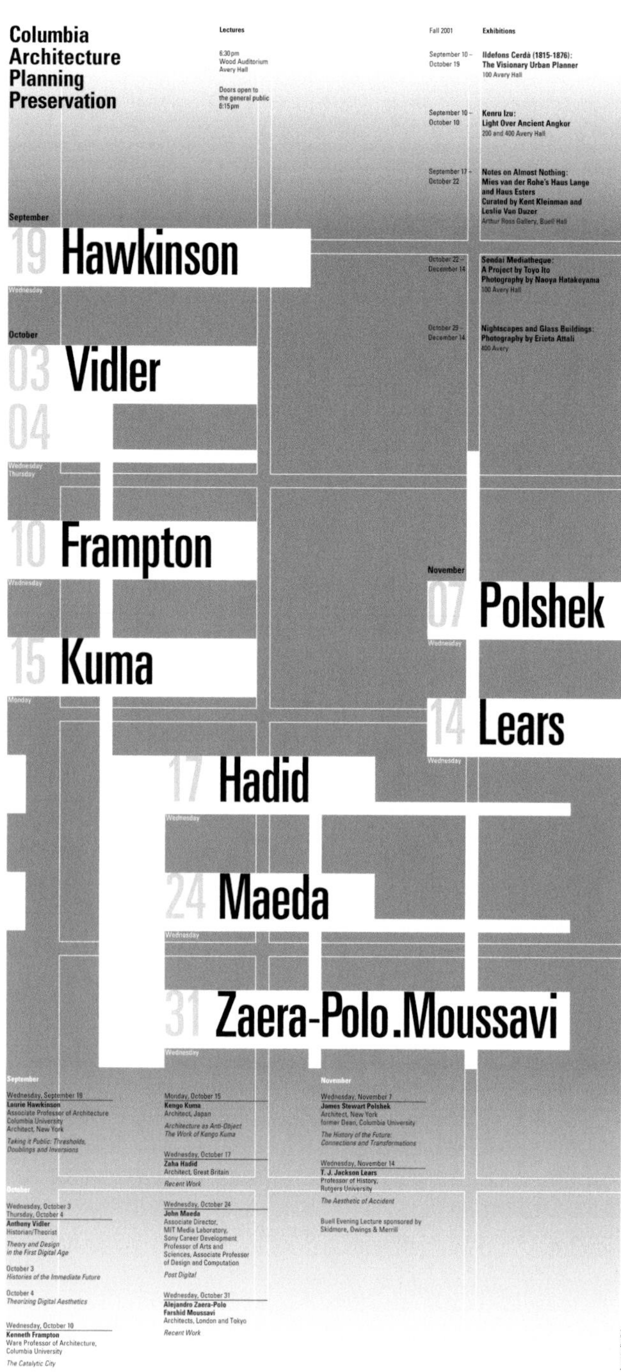

12 x 24 in.

Poster announcing a series of nine lectures and five exhibitions held over a three-month period at the Columbia University Graduate School of Architecture, Planning and Preservation.

Concept: to suggest a dense urban fabric. The lectures are arranged counter-clockwise, starting on the top left.

The topology comprises four optical levels: the lecturers' names, the secondary information, the 3x6 unit grid, and the tonal background with windows.

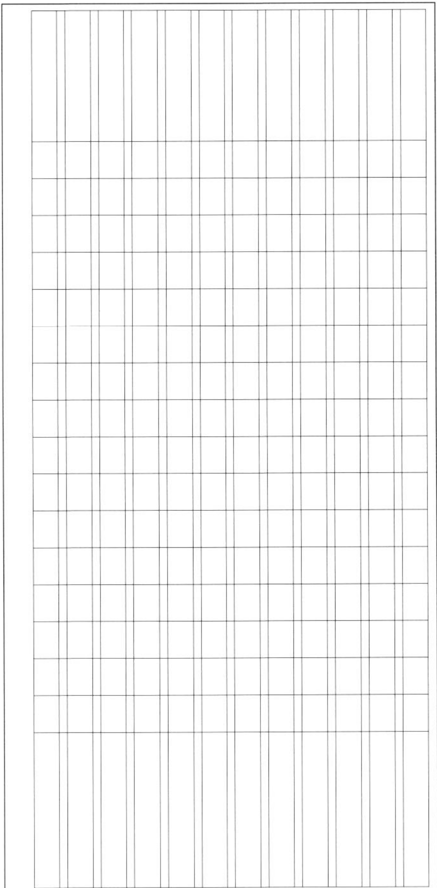

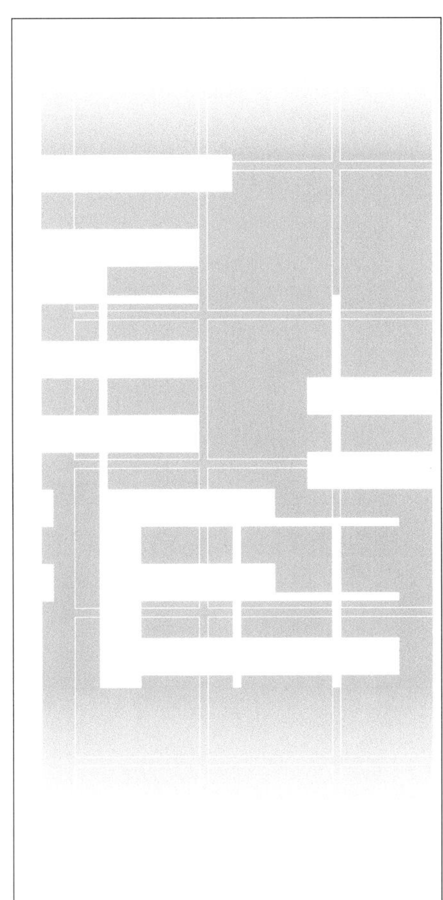

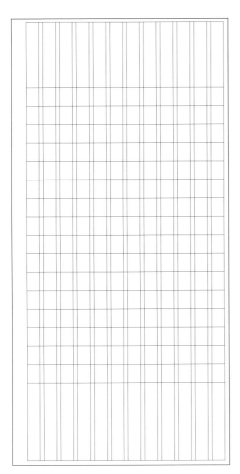

The primary structure, consisting of 12 columns and 16 rows, positions the typographic information.

The secondary structure, consisting of 3x6 square units, partially determines the background windows. The three horizontal units correspond with the 12 columns of the primary structure.

The background windows derive from a combination of the primary and the secondary structure.

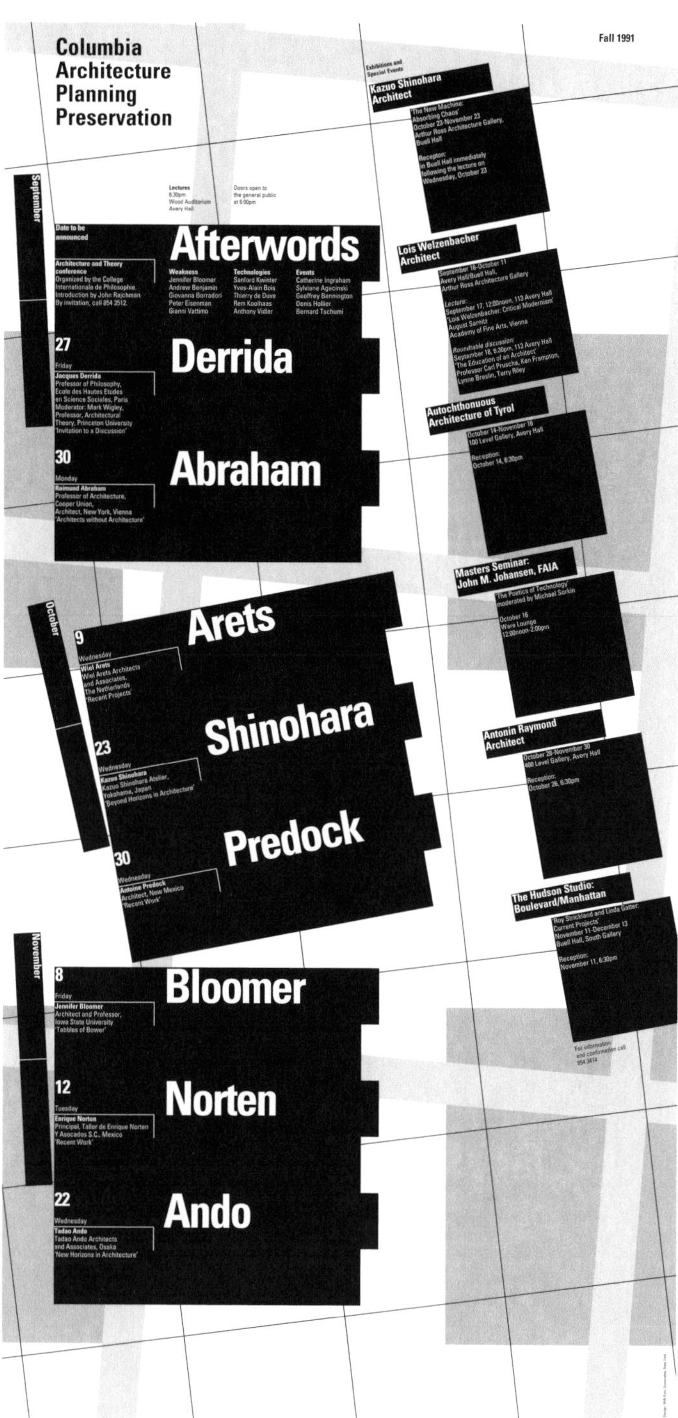

12 x 24 in.

Poster announcing a series of nine lectures and six exhibitions held over a three-month period at the Columbia University Graduate School of Architecture, Planning and Preservation.

Concept: to suggest an assemblage of industrial materials. The 3:3:3 ratios of lectures per month determine the theme of the three large squares. The exhibitions are grouped in a column of six small squares.

The topology comprises four optical levels: the squares with lectures and exhibitions, the squares in the background, the bold grid, and the light grid.

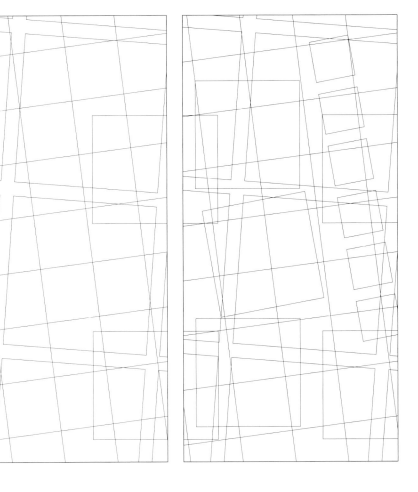

Diagram of the primary optical level. The large square in the middle and the column of six small squares are rotated counter clock-wise for contrast.

Square-based grids of different scale create the secondary levels and add depth to the composition by establishing a fore-, middle-, and background.

Diagram of the four optical levels. All elements are square-based. To avoid optical clusters, each level's angle was determined in diagrammatic form.

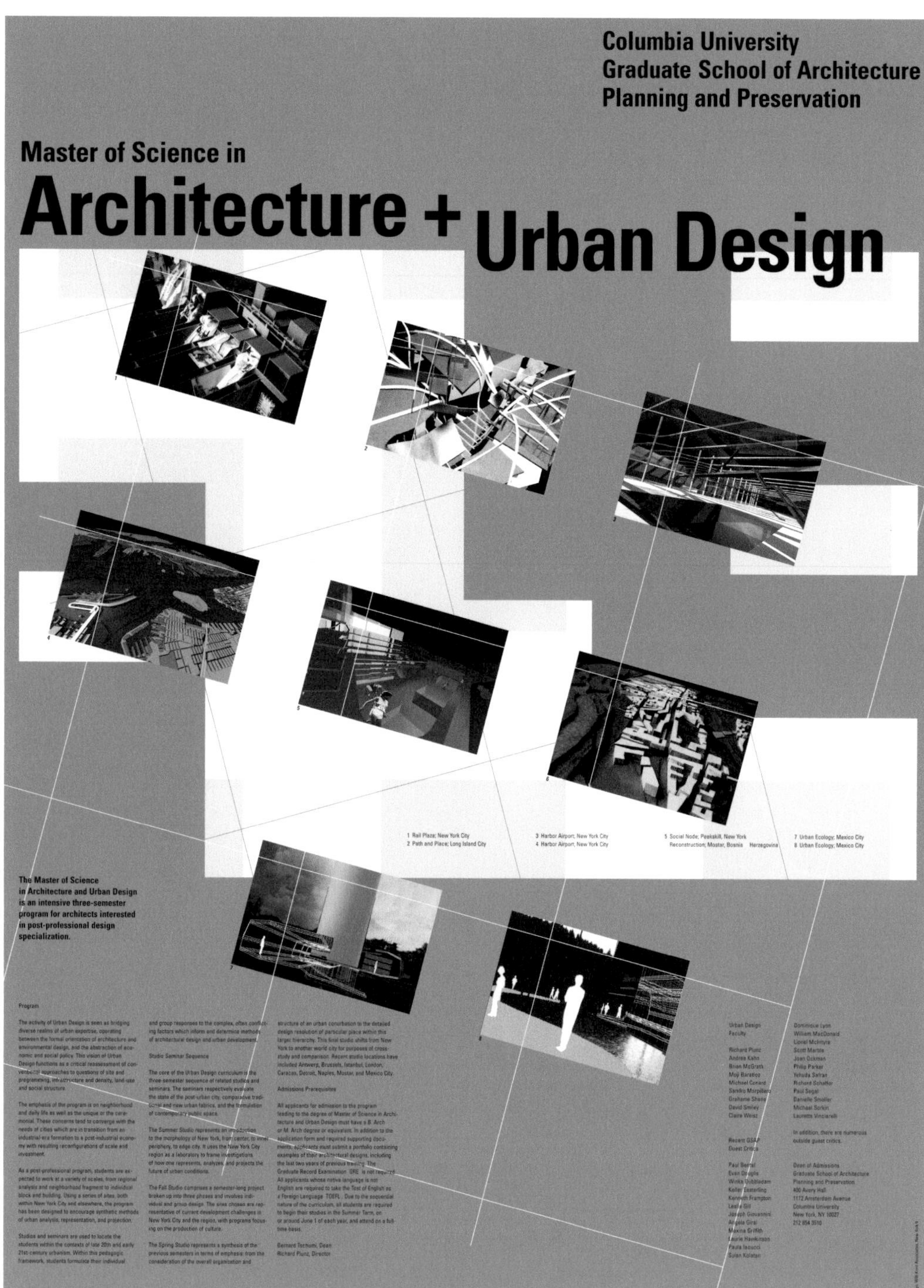

18 x 24 in.

Poster announcing a graduate program in architecture and urban design at the Columbia University Graduate School of Architecture, Planning and Preservation.

Concept: To convey the field of study through a series of photographs of student work.

The topology comprises six optical levels: the typographic information, the photographs, the grids in front and in the back of the photographs, the background with windows, and the gray squares in the back.

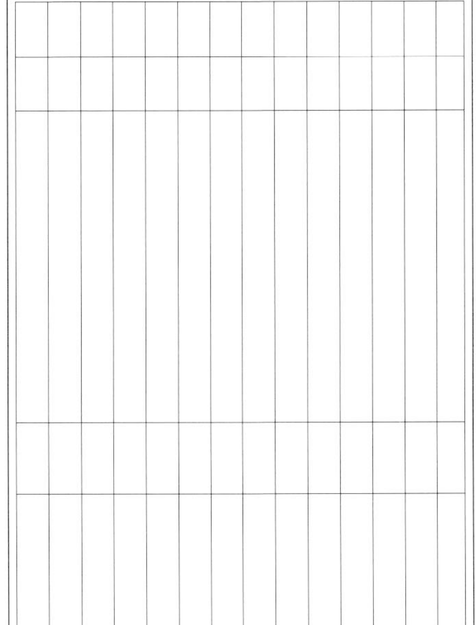

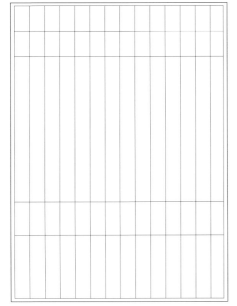

Diagram of typographic information. Four horizontal alignments intersect with fourteen columns.

Composite diagram. The fine-line grids are rotated 15 degrees clock- and counter-clockwise to contrast with the nine solid squares. The photographs, proportioned 3:2, are the intermediaries between the solid squares and the fine-line grid. The width of the photographs corresponds to the width of the solid squares.

Windows, revealing parts of optical level one, evoke visual depth.

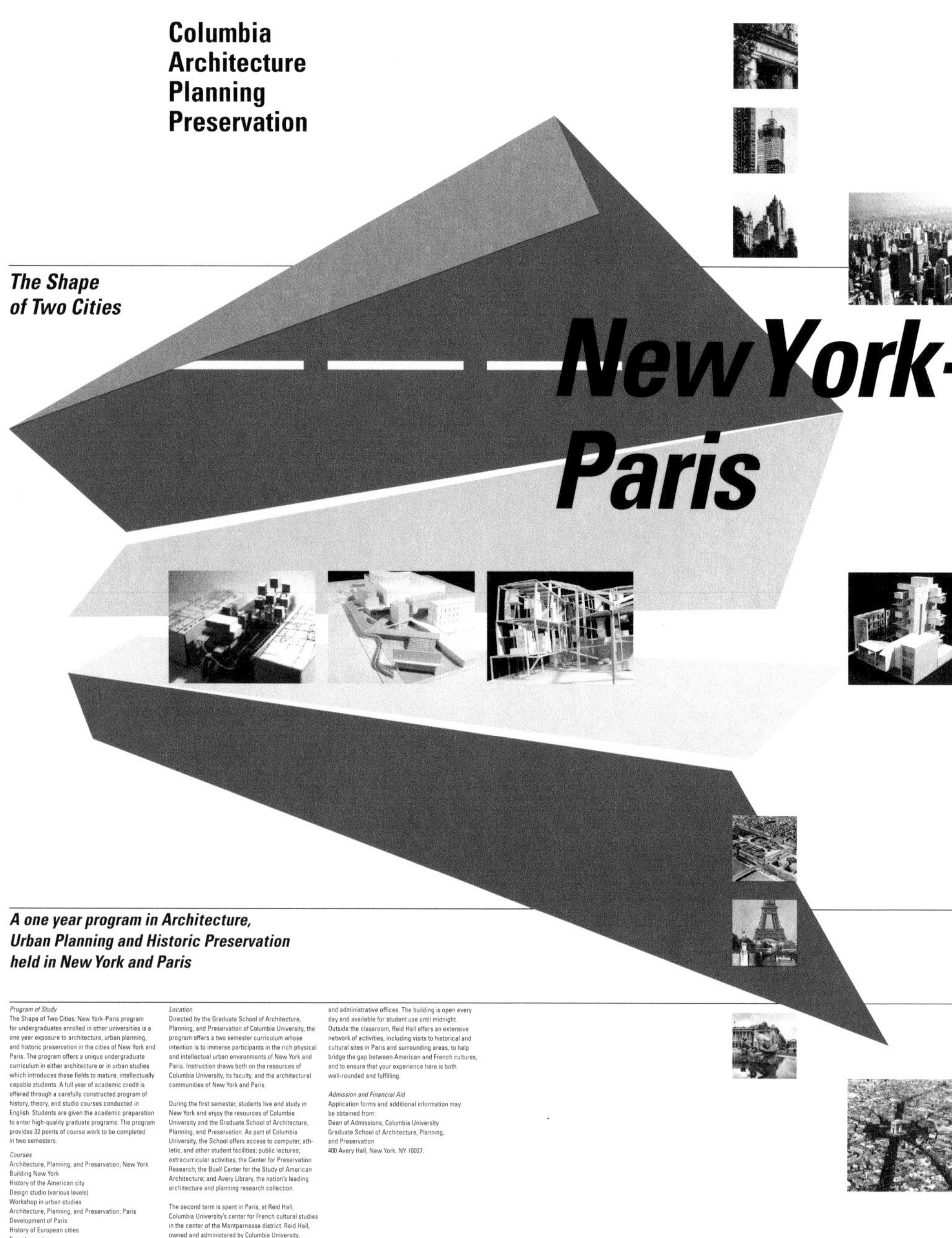

Columbia
Architecture
Planning
Preservation
The Shape
of Two Cities
New York-
Paris
A one year program in Architecture,
Urban Planning and Historic Preservation
held in New York and Paris
Program of Study
The Shape of Two Cities: New York-Paris program for undergraduates enrolled in other universities is a one year exposure to architecture, urban planning, and historic preservation in the cities of New York and Paris. The program offers a unique undergraduate curriculum in either architecture or in urban studies which introduces these fields to mature, intellectually capable students. A full year of academic credit is offered through a carefully constructed program of history, theory, and studio courses conducted in English. Students are given the academic preparation to enter high-quality graduate programs. The program provides 32 points of course work to be completed in two semesters.
Courses
Architecture, Planning, and Preservation; New York
Building New York
History of the American city
Design studio (various levels)
Workshop in urban studies
Architecture, Planning, and Preservation; Paris
Development of Paris
History of European cities
French seminar
plus Electives
Location
Directed by the Graduate School of Architecture, Planning, and Preservation of Columbia University, the program offers a two semester curriculum whose intention is to immerse participants in the rich physical and intellectual urban environments of New York and Paris. Instruction draws both on the resources of Columbia University, its faculty, and the architectural communities of New York and Paris.
During the first semester, students live and study in New York and enjoy the resources of Columbia University and the Graduate School of Architecture, Planning, and Preservation. As part of Columbia University, the School offers access to computer, athletic, and other student facilities; public lectures; extracurricular activities; the Center for Preservation Research; the Buell Center for the Study of American Architecture; and Avery Library, the nation's leading architecture and planning research collection.
The second term is spent in Paris, at Reid Hall, Columbia University's center for French cultural studies in the center of the Montparnasse district. Reid Hall, owned and administered by Columbia University, is located on the rue de Chevreuse near the Luxembourg gardens. The original building was constructed in the early 18th century; modern additions have enlarged the facility, creating an interior courtyard and private garden. Reid Hall has a 4000-volume library, classrooms, a reading and computer room, lounges, and administrative offices. The building is open every day and available for student use until midnight. Outside the classroom, Reid Hall offers an extensive network of activities, including visits to historical and cultural sites in Paris and surrounding areas, to help bridge the gap between American and French cultures, and to ensure that your experience here is both well-rounded and fulfilling.
Admission and Financial Aid
Application forms and additional information may be obtained from:
Dean of Admissions, Columbia University
Graduate School of Architecture, Planning, and Preservation
400 Avery Hall, New York, NY 10027.

18×24 in.

Poster announcing an undergraduate program in architecture, urban planning, and historic preservation held in New York and Paris

Concept: To convey the program's multifaceted character by combining student work with photographs of the course locations, New York City and Paris.

The topology comprises three optical levels: the typographic information, the central folded form that attracts the reader's attention, and a series of horizontally and vertically aligned photographs.

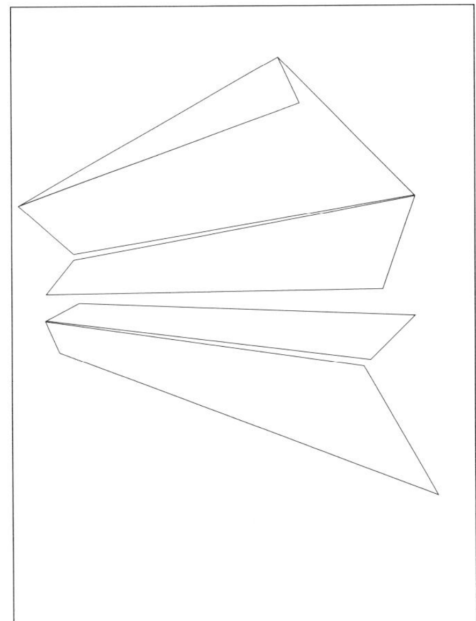

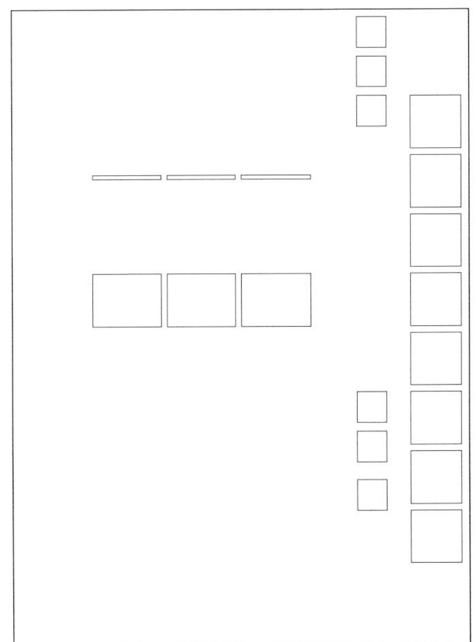

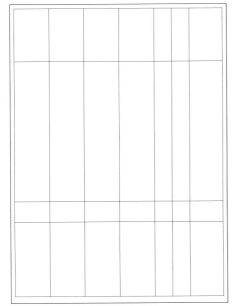

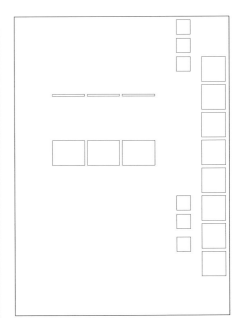

Diagram of typographic information. Three horizontal alignments intersect with seven columns.

Diagram of the folded form. The form contrasts with orthogonal levels one and three.

Diagram of photographs contrasting in shape and size. The column on the right is left complete to show the full sequence of the photographs.

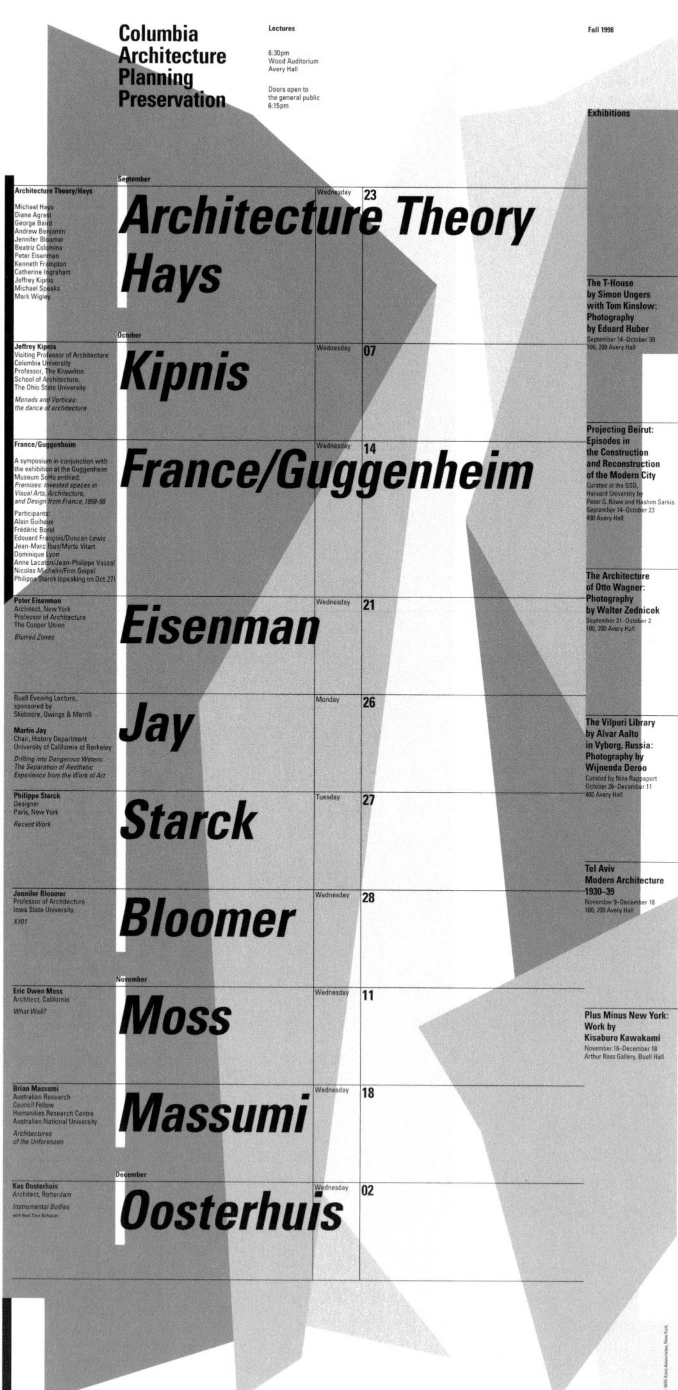

12x24 in.

Poster announcing a series of ten lectures and six exhibitions held over a four-month period at the Columbia University Graduate School of Architecture, Planning and Preservation.

Concept: To express the lectures' architectural themes by juxtaposing the typographic information with implied three-dimensional forms. The extreme differences in length of lecture titles and the large amount of secondary information determine the typographic structure.

The topology comprises three optical levels: the lecture titles, the exhibition and lecture information, and the free forms suggesting additional optical levels.

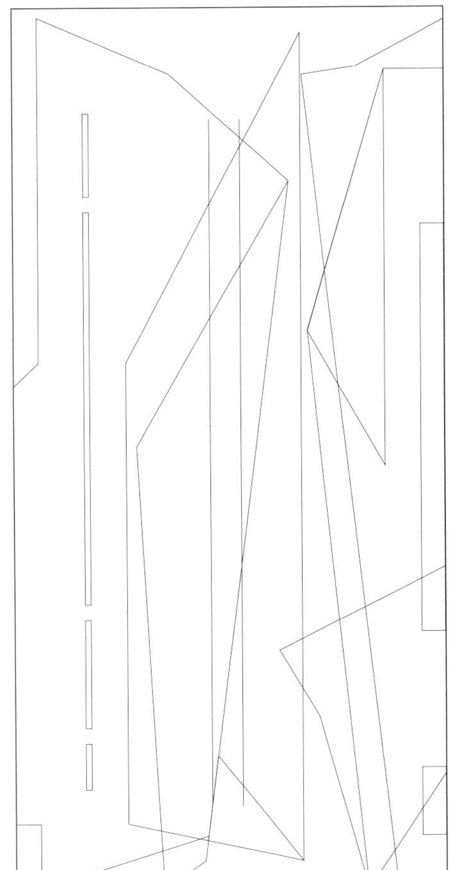

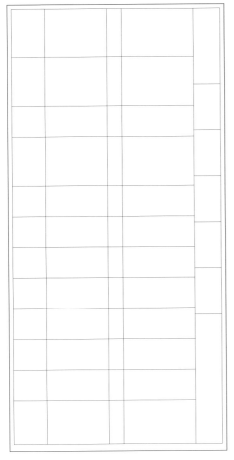

Diagram of typographic information. The length of titles and secondary information determine both the vertical alignments and the horizontal subdivisions.

Diagram of the background level. The composition started with the large form on the left as a unifying element for the lectures. The exhibitions on the right are placed against a series of active smaller forms. All forms were developed step-by-step, responding to the initial form and gradually leading to the final composition.

The background design. Dividing the poster into a large area for the lectures on the left and a smaller area for the exhibitions on the right creates additional optical levels.

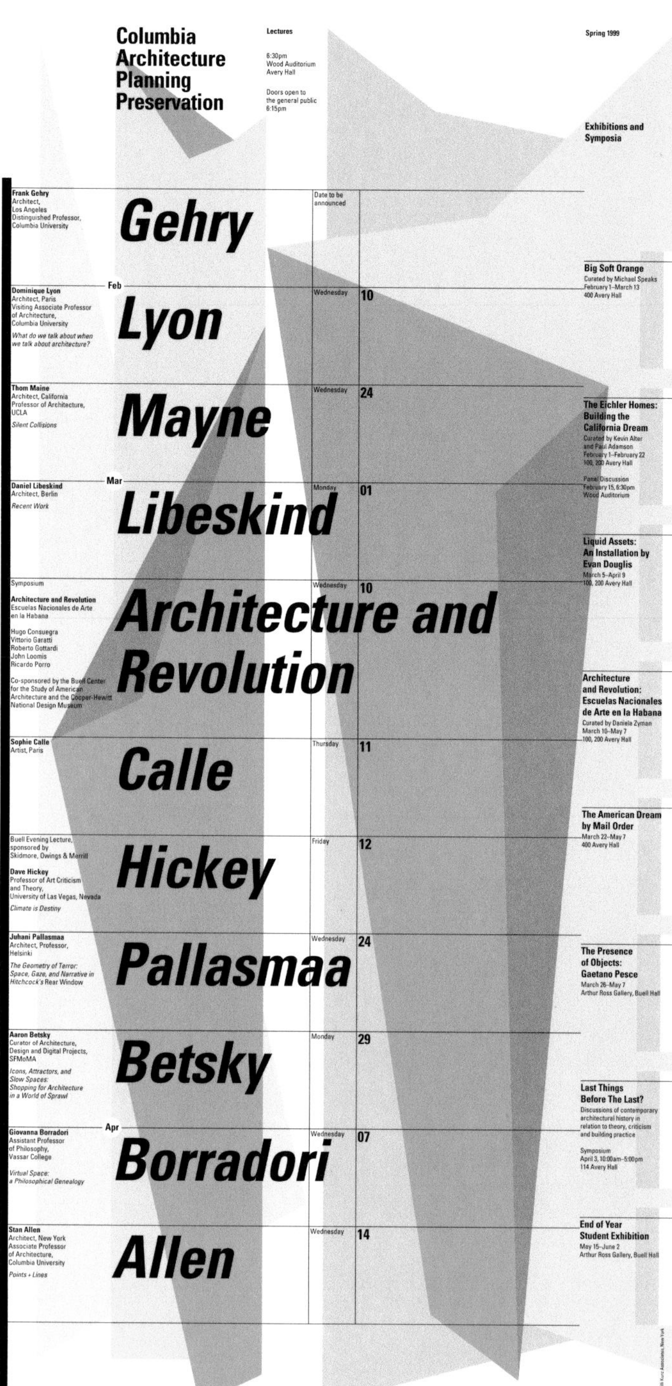

12 x 24 in.

Poster announcing a series of eleven lectures and six exhibitions held over a four-month period at the Columbia University Graduate School of Architecture, Planning and Preservation.

Concept: To express the lectures' architectural themes by juxtaposing the typographic information with implied three-dimensional forms. The extreme differences in length of lecture titles and the large amount of secondary information determine the typographic structure.

The topology comprises three optical levels: the lecture titles, the exhibition and lecture information, and the free forms suggesting additional optical levels.

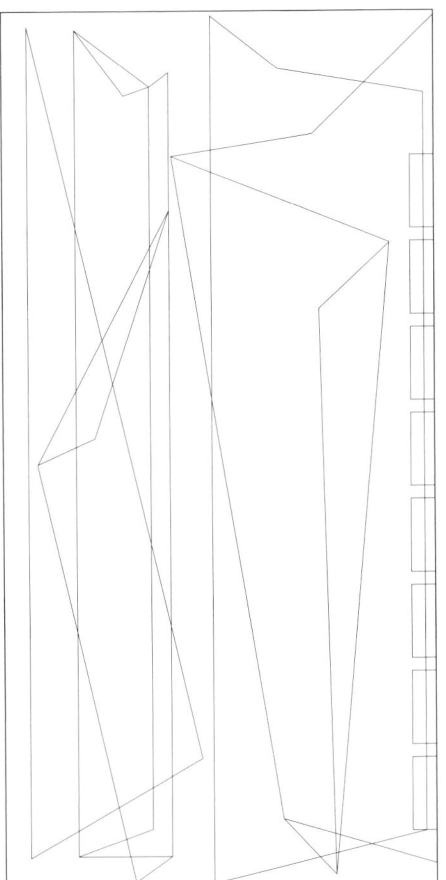

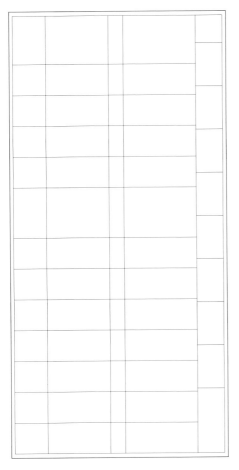

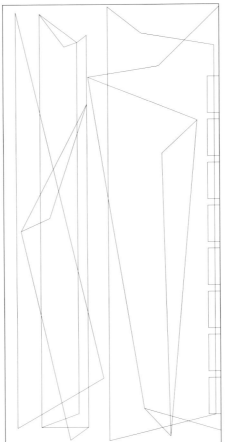

Diagram of typographic information. The length of titles and the secondary information determine both the vertical alignments and the horizontal subdivisions.

Diagram of the background level. The composition started with the large form on the right defining the position of the exhibitions. The lectures on the left are placed against a series of active narrow forms. All forms were developed step-by-step, responding to the initial form and gradually leading to the final composition.

The background design. Dividing the poster into a small area for the lectures on the left and a larger area for the exhibitions on the right creates additional optical levels.

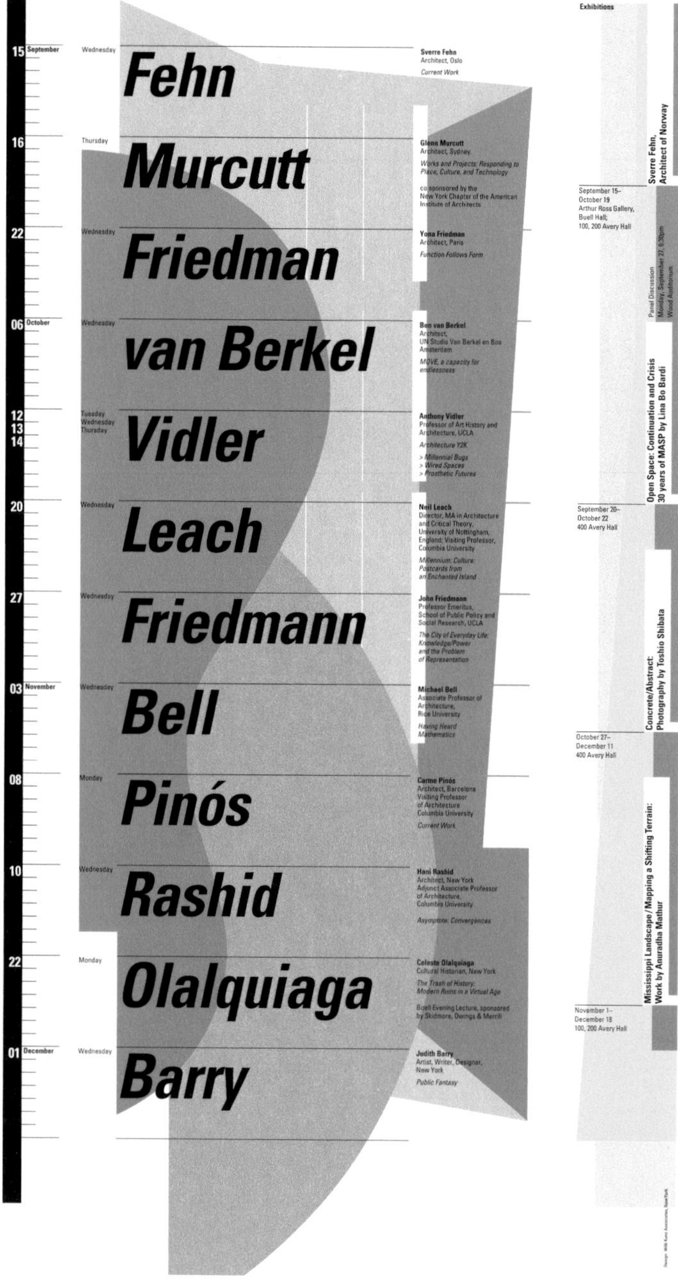

12 x 24 in.

Poster announcing a series of twelve lectures and four exhibitions held over a four-month period at the Columbia University Graduate School of Architecture, Planning and Preservation.

Concept: To express the lectures' architectural themes by juxtaposing the typographic information with a collage of geometric and curvilinear forms. The dense block of lecture information on the left contrasts with the loose exhibition listing on the right.

The topology comprises five optical levels: the lecture titles, the lecture and exhibition information, and the three-level background.

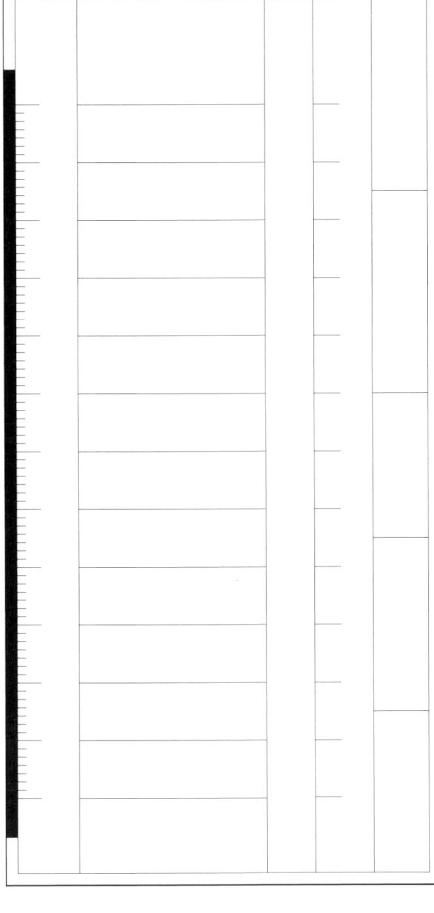

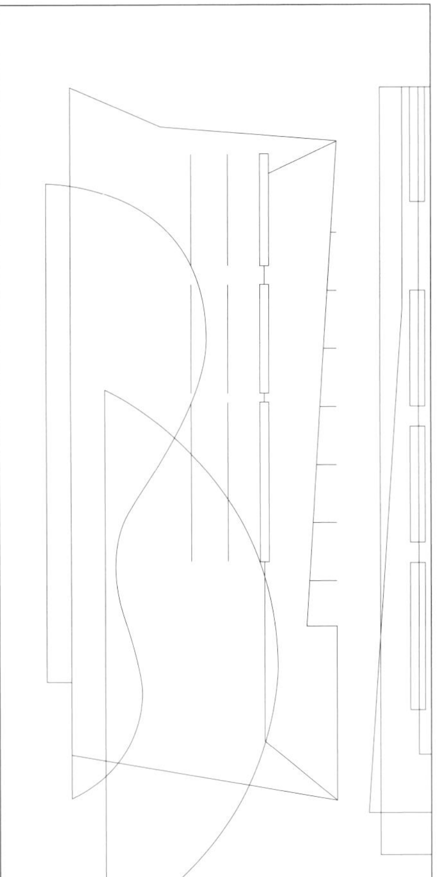

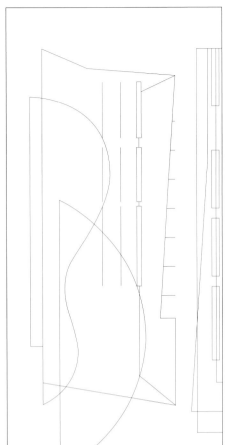

Diagram of typographic information. The length of titles and the secondary information determine both the vertical alignments and the horizontal subdivisions. The scale along the left-hand edge signifies the progression of time.

Diagram of the background levels. The large geometric form in the background was developed first. The intersecting curvilinear forms of levels two and three contrast with the geometric background form.

Composite of the three background levels. Contrast between curvilinear and rectilinear forms.

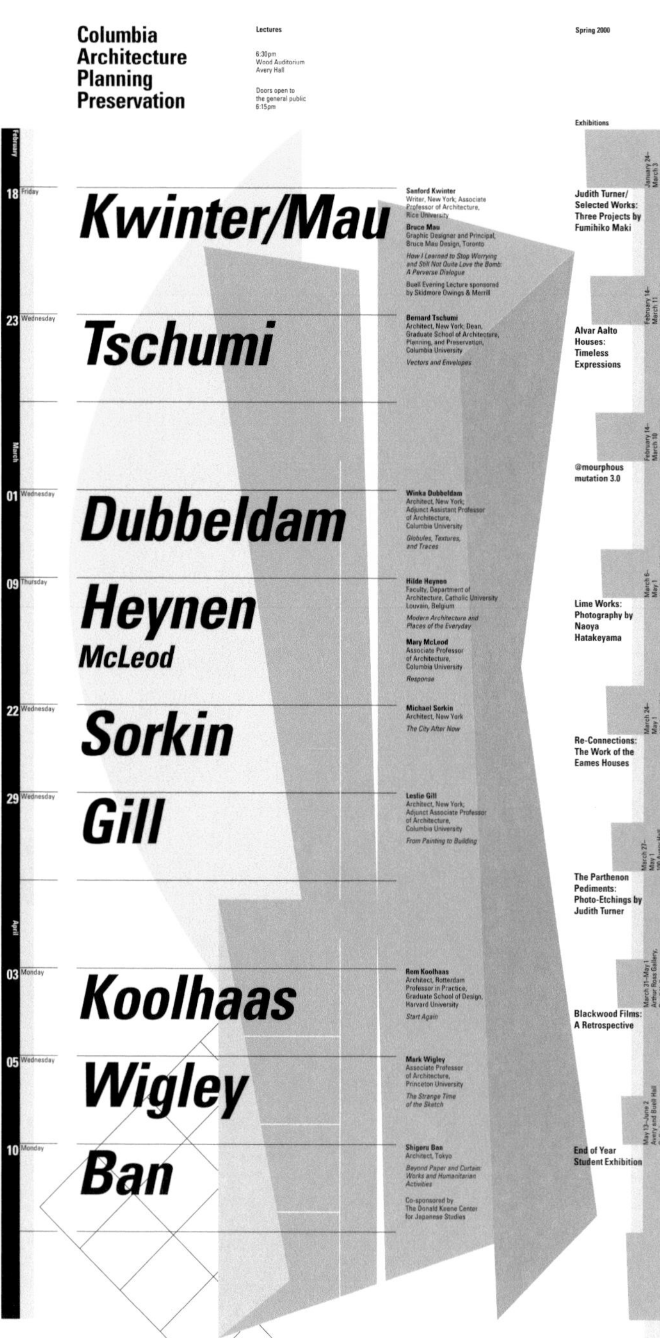

12 x 24 in.

Poster announcing a series of nine lectures and eight exhibitions held over a three-month period at the Columbia University Graduate School of Architecture, Planning and Preservation.

Concept: To express the lectures' architectural themes by juxtaposing the typographic information with a collage of geometric elements. The lecturers' names are grouped according to month.

The topology comprises six optical levels: the lecture titles, the lecture and exhibition information, and the four-level background.

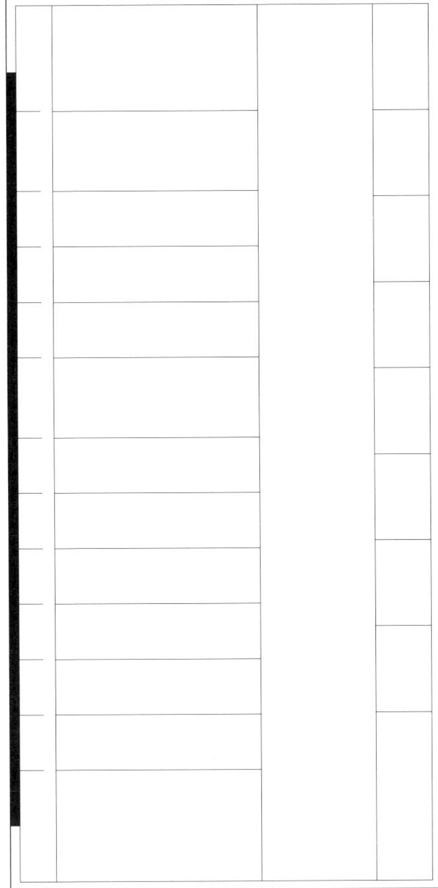

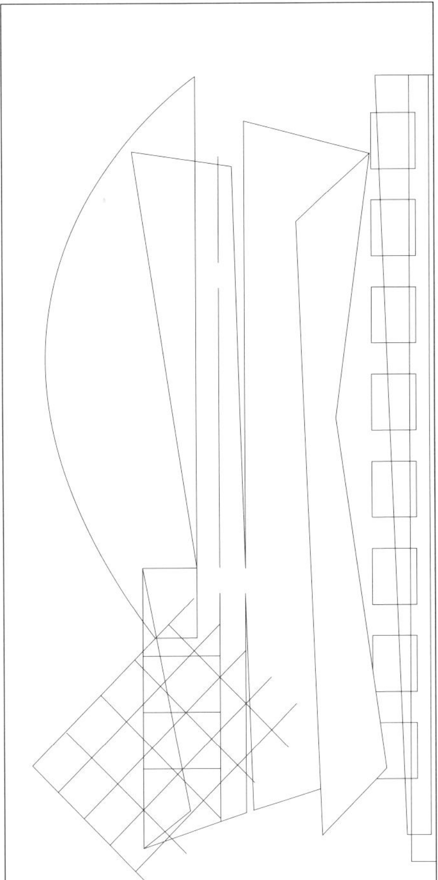

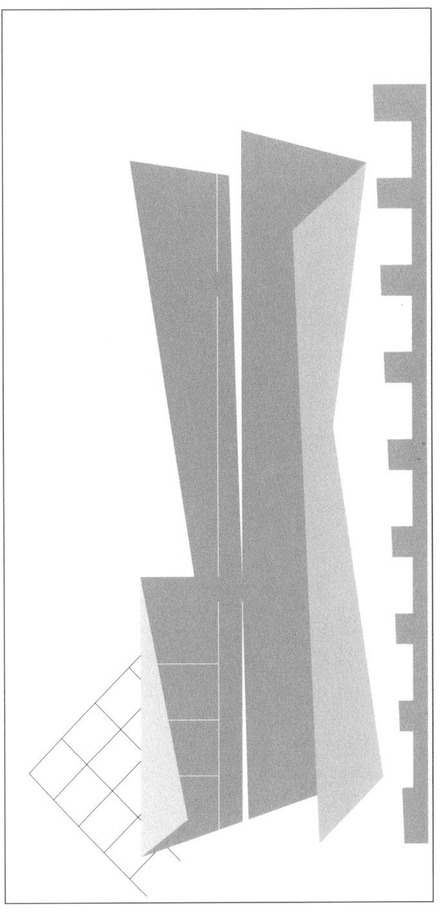

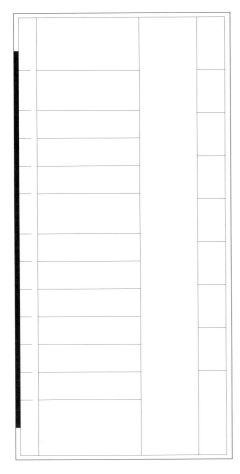

Diagram of typographic information. The titles' length and the secondary information determine both the vertical alignments and the horizontal subdivisions.

Diagram of the background levels. The large geometric form was developed first. The curvilinear form and the tilted orthogonal grid contrast with the large geometric form.

Composite of the four background levels contrasting in form and optical weight.

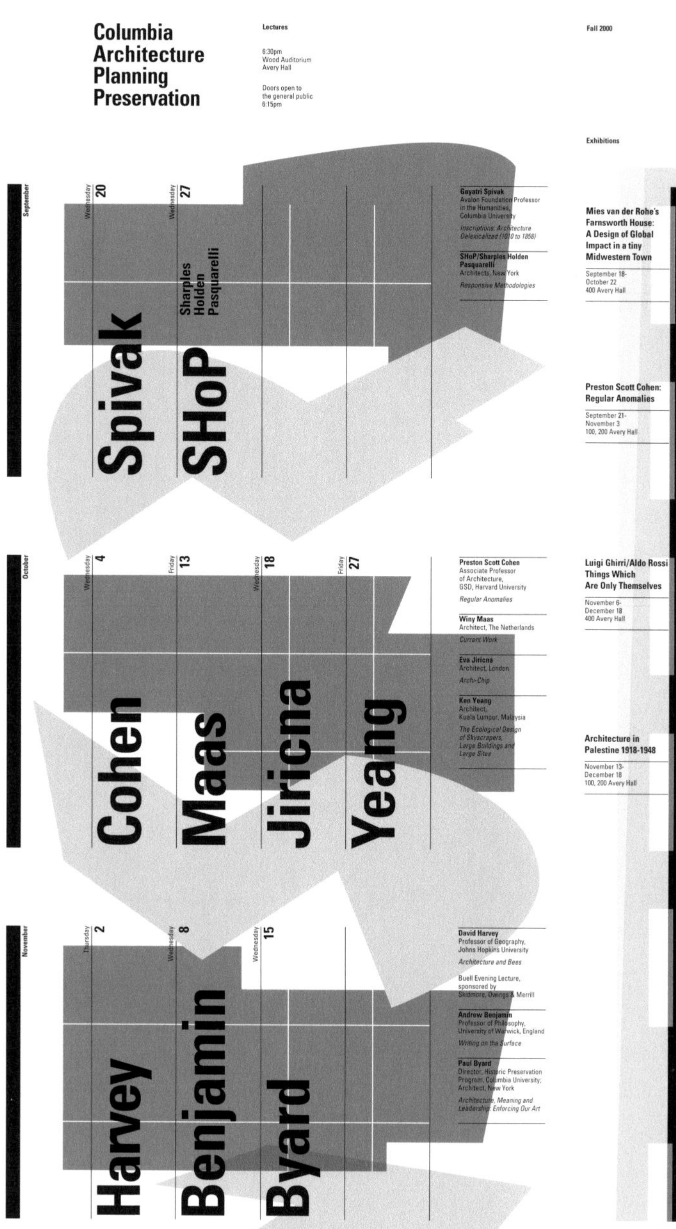

Columbia
Architecture
Planning
Preservation
Lectures
6:30pm
Wood Auditorium
Avery Hall
Doors open to
the general public
6:15pm
Fall 2000
Exhibitions
Spivak
SHoP
Sharples
Holden
Pasquarelli
Cohen
Maas
Jiricna
Yeang
Harvey
Benjamin
Byard
Mies van der Rohe's
Farnsworth House:
A Design of Global
Impact in a tiny
Midwestern Town
Preston Scott Cohen:
Regular Anomalies
Luigi Ghirri/Aldo Rossi
Things Which
Are Only Themselves
Architecture in
Palestine 1918-1948

12 x 24 in.

Poster announcing a series of nine lectures and four exhibitions held over a three-month period at the Columbia University Graduate School of Architecture, Planning and Preservation.

Concept: To distinguish each of the three lecture groups with a pair of distinct graphic elements – a two-dimensional form combined with one suggesting a third dimension. The titles are positioned vertically for contrast.

The topology comprises four optical levels: the lecture titles, the lecture and exhibition information, and the two-tier shapes in the background.

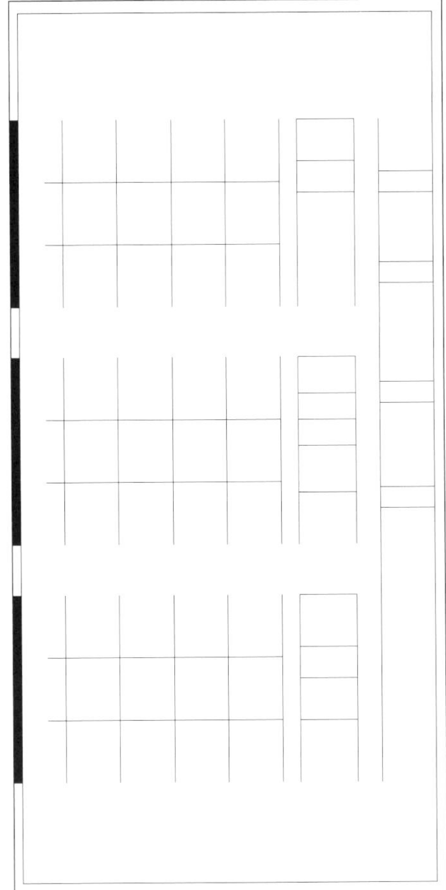

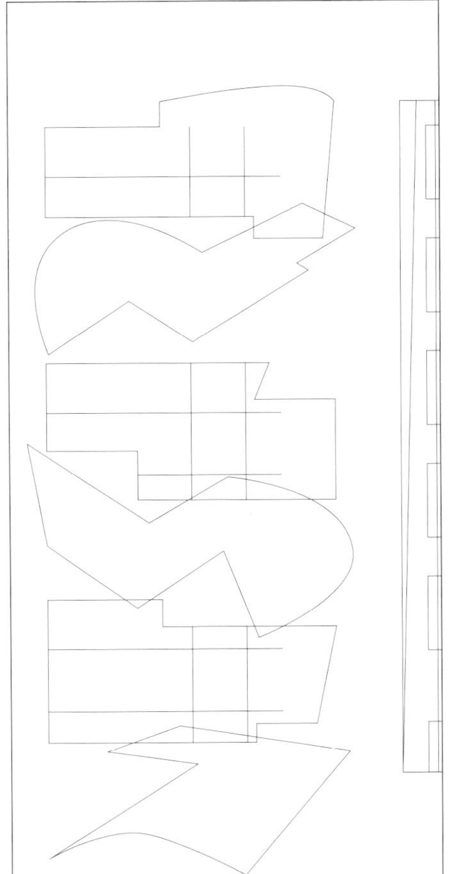

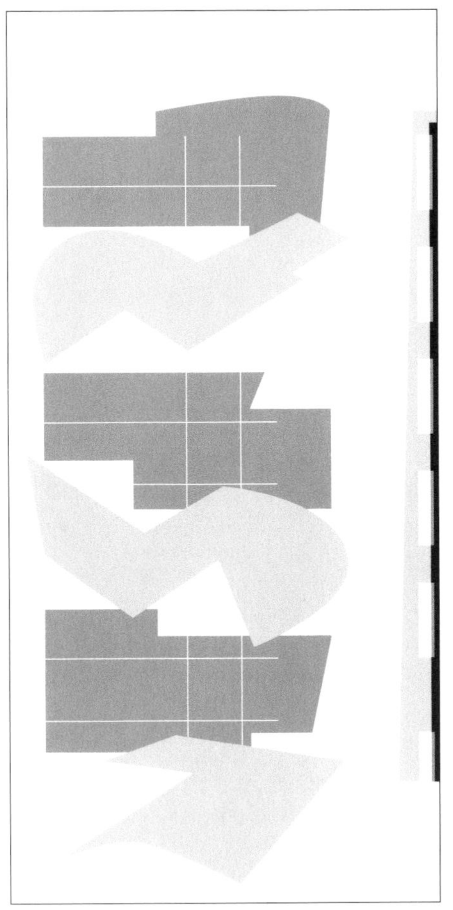

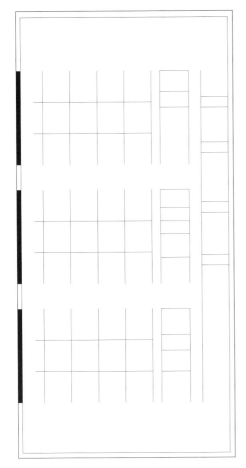

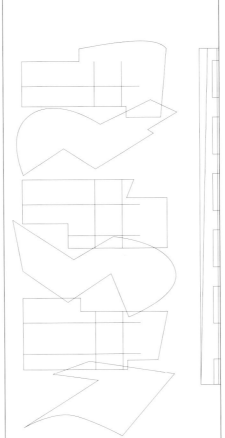

Diagram of typographic information. The strong orthogonal layout contrasts with the dynamic composition of the background levels.

Diagram of background levels. The optically three-dimensional forms were developed as intermediaries between the flat forms.

Composite of the background levels. The optically three-dimensional forms appear to float in front of the flat forms.

Glossary

A

a priori: conceived or established before analysis, investigation or experience.
ambiguous: having more than one possible meaning or interpretation.
ambivalence: the presence of two opposing ideas, attitudes, or emotions at the same time.
analysis: separation of an element into its component parts; the close examination of something in order to understand it better or draw conclusions from it.
atomize: to separate into small components.

C

cognition: the mental faculty or process of acquiring knowledge through reasoning, intuition or perception.
comprehension: the ability to grasp the meaning of something.
concept: an abstract idea or guiding principle derived from particular conditions or context.
congruent: corresponding to or consistent with each other.
connotation: the suggesting of a meaning by a word apart from the thing it explicitly names or describes.
context: the physical and cultural environment in which typography functions and by which it is conditioned.
cue: a signal or stimulus, often subconsciously perceived, that results in a specific behavioral response.

D

diagram: a line drawing that describes the organization, structure, function, and relationships of elements.
disposition: prevailing tendency or mood, or inclination to act in a particular way.
divergent: following a course differing from the typical path.

E

effect: a distinctive impression to bring about a change or action.
empirical: relying on personal experience or observation, often without due regard for a system or theory.
equilibrium: a static or dynamic balance between opposing elements or forces.
explicit: characterized by clear expression, fully developed or formulated.
expression: felicitous or vivid indication or depiction of a mood or sentiment.

F

function: the action for which a thing is specially fitted or used or for which a thing exists.

G

grid: a network of uniformly spaced horizontal and vertical lines for positioning typographic elements.

H

hierarchy: arrangement of elements into a graded series.
hybrid: something made up of a mixture of different elements.

I

indexical: serving as a pointer or indicator.
idiosyncrasy: the special characteristics that make something distinct.
information: the communication or reception of knowledge obtained from investigation, study, or instruction.
integral: being an essential part of something or any of the parts that make up a whole.
intermediary: an element that establishes an optical connection; an in-between element.
intrinsic: belonging to the essential nature or constitution of something.

L

legibility: clarity and efficiency in reading.

M

mnemonic: assisting or intended to assist memory; acting as a memory aid.

O

orthogonal: relating to or composed of right angles.

P

position: the place of an element in relation to the space or to other elements, e.g., the position of a letter within a word.
principle: a comprehensive and fundamental law or assumption; the underlying facts of how something works; a standard of moral or ethical decision-making.
process: a series of actions or steps that lead toward a particular result.

R

readability: pleasure and interest in reading.
repertoire: the complete range of techniques, abilities, or skills possessed by a person.
resonance: the effect of a design beyond its immediate surface meaning.

S

semantics: the meaning or the differences between meanings of words or symbols.
status quo: the existing state of affairs.
subliminal: entering, existing in, or affecting the mind without conscious awareness.
syntax: the way in which words are put together to form phrases and sentences.
synthesis: the composition or combination of parts or elements so as to form a whole.

T

theory: a body of principles presenting a concise, systematic view of a subject.
thesis: a proposition advanced as an argument.
topology: the science, knowledge, or study of place, position, and arrangement.
transition: passage from one place, subject, or condition to another.

Recommended reading

B

Bill, Max
Typography, advertising, book design
Sulgen, Switzerland: Verlag Niggli AG
1999

Bosshard, Hans Rudolf
The typographic grid
Sulgen, Switzerland: Verlag Niggli AG
2000

Burke, Christopher
Paul Renner: the art of typography
New York:
Princeton Architectural Press
1998

C

Cohen, Arthur A.
Herbert Bayer
Cambridge, MA: MIT Press
1984

G

Gerstner, Karl
Compendium for literates
Cambridge, MA: MIT Press
1974

Gerstner, Karl
Designing programmes
Teufen, Switzerland: Arthur Niggli Ltd.
1964

Gill, Eric
An essay on typography
Boston: David R. Godine, Publisher
1988

H

Hiebert, Kenneth
Graphic design process
New York: Van Nostrand Reinhold
1992

Hochuli, Jost; Kinross Robin
Designing books: practice and theory
London: Hyphen Press
1996

Hofmann, Armin
Graphic design manual
Sulgen, Switzerland: Verlag Niggli AG
1988

K

Kepes, Gyorgy
Language of vision
Chicago: Paul Theobald
1944

Kepes, Gyorgy, ed.
Education of vision
New York: George Braziller, Inc.
1965

Kepes, Gyorgy, ed.
Sign, image, symbol
New York: George Braziller, Inc.
1966

Kinross, Robin
Modern typography
London: Hyphen Press
1992

Kinross, Robin
Anthony Froshaug: typography & texts
London: Hyphen Press
2000

Kinross, Robin
Anthony Froshaug: documents of a life
London: Hyphen Press
2000

Kinross, Robin
Unjustified texts
London: Hyphen Press
2002

Kröplien, Manfred, ed.
Karl Gerstner
Ostfildern-Ruit: Hatje Cantz Verlag
2001

Kunz, Willi
Typography: Macro- and
Microaesthetics
Sulgen, Switzerland: Verlag Niggli AG
2002

L

Le Corbusier
The Modulor 1; the Modulor 2
Cambridge: Harvard University Press
1980

M

Meggs, Philip
A history of graphic design
New York: Van Nostrand Reinhold
1992

Moholy-Nagy, Sibyl
Moholy-Nagy, experiment in totality
Cambridge, MA: MIT Press
1969

Müller-Brockmann, Josef
Grid systems
Sulgen, Switzerland: Verlag Niggli AG
1988

R

Rand, Paul
A designer's art
New Haven: Yale University Press
1985

Ruder, Emil
Typography
Sulgen, Switzerland: Verlag Niggli AG
2002

T

Tschichold, Jan
Asymmetric typography
New York: Reinhold Publishing
1967

Tschichold, Jan
The new typography
Berkley: University of California Press
1995

W

Weingart, Wolfgang
My way to typography
Baden, Switzerland:
Lars Müller Publishers
2000

Wittgenstein, Ludwig
Tractatus logico-philosophicus
London: Routledge
1981

Z

Zwimpfer, Moritz
Visual perception
Sulgen, Switzerland: Verlag Niggli AG
1994

Index

Photo credits
Page 73
Kim Keever, New York
Page 131, top left
Elliott Erwitt/Magnum Photos

Illustrative texts on pages
52-57, 77, 79, 83-85, and 87
are from the essay *The Moving Eye*
by Jacqueline Tyrwhitt
in *Explorations in Communication,*
Edmund Carpenter,
Marshall McLuhan, eds.

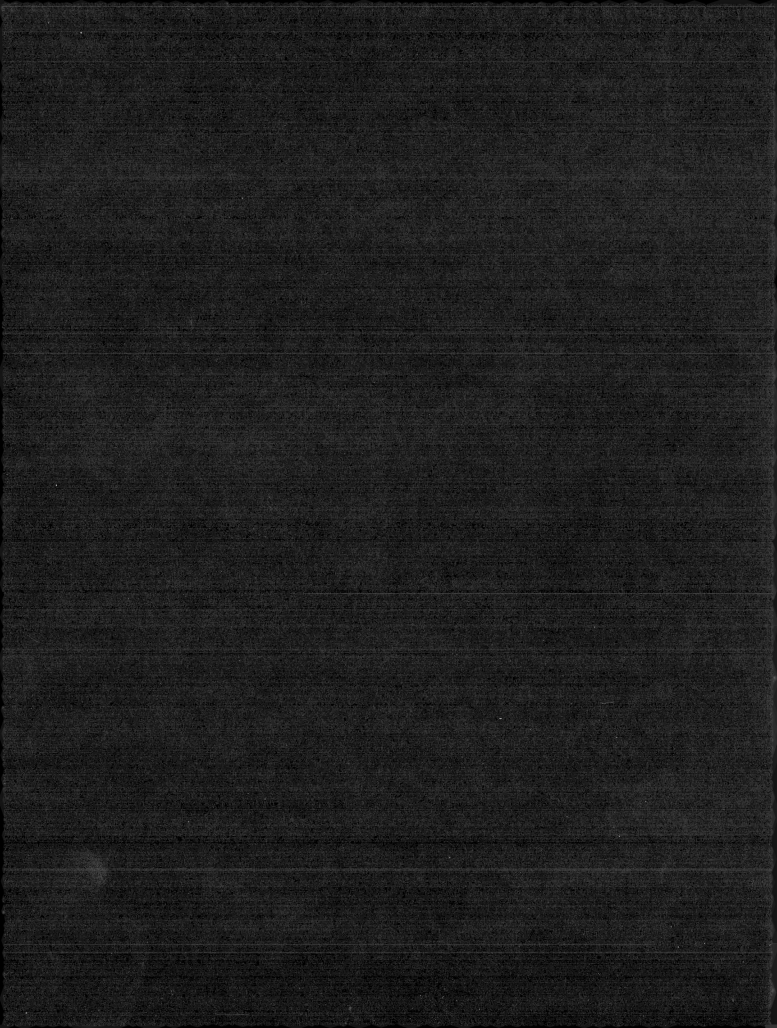